Addition

Name _____

Total Problems	23
Problems Correct	_____

$$\begin{array}{r} 1 \\ +3 \\ \hline \end{array} \qquad \begin{array}{r} 2 \\ +4 \\ \hline \end{array}$$

$$\begin{array}{r} 0 \\ +5 \\ \hline \end{array} \quad \begin{array}{r} 3 \\ +2 \\ \hline \end{array} \quad \begin{array}{r} 0 \\ +0 \\ \hline \end{array} \quad \begin{array}{r} 5 \\ +1 \\ \hline \end{array} \quad \begin{array}{r} 2 \\ +2 \\ \hline \end{array}$$

$$\begin{array}{r} 1 \\ +1 \\ \hline \end{array} \quad \begin{array}{r} 4 \\ +1 \\ \hline \end{array} \quad \begin{array}{r} 3 \\ +3 \\ \hline \end{array} \quad \begin{array}{r} 2 \\ +1 \\ \hline \end{array} \quad \begin{array}{r} 0 \\ +6 \\ \hline \end{array}$$

$$\begin{array}{r} 3 \\ +1 \\ \hline \end{array} \quad \begin{array}{r} 5 \\ +0 \\ \hline \end{array} \quad \begin{array}{r} 4 \\ +2 \\ \hline \end{array} \quad \begin{array}{r} 3 \\ +0 \\ \hline \end{array} \quad \begin{array}{r} 1 \\ +5 \\ \hline \end{array}$$

$$\begin{array}{r} 4 \\ +0 \\ \hline \end{array} \quad \begin{array}{r} 1 \\ +2 \\ \hline \end{array} \quad \begin{array}{r} 6 \\ +0 \\ \hline \end{array}$$

With practice, you can do it!

$$\begin{array}{r} 0 \\ +2 \\ \hline \end{array} \quad \begin{array}{r} 2 \\ +3 \\ \hline \end{array} \quad \begin{array}{r} 3 \\ +0 \\ \hline \end{array}$$

Math IF8739

1

Addition

Name _____

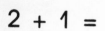

Total Problems	30
Problems Correct	_____

2 + 1 =

4 + 0 =

1 + 2 =   0 + 6 =   0 + 5 =

6 + 0 =   3 + 2 =   2 + 4 =

1 + 4 =   0 + 0 =   1 + 3 =

0 + 3 =   2 + 3 =   0 + 2 =

3 + 1 =   5 + 1 =   2 + 1 =

5 + 0 =   2 + 0 =   4 + 1 =

4 + 2 =   6 + 0 =   0 + 4 =

2 + 3 =   2 + 2 =   5 + 1 =

Practice = Success!

1 + 1 =   1 + 5 =

3 + 3 =   3 + 0 =

Addition

Name _____

| Total Problems | 25 |
| Problems Correct | _____ |

```
  4        0
 +2       +7
```

```
  2        4        5        2        5
 +3       +3       +1       +4       +2
```

```
  6        2        5        3        2
 +0       +2       +0       +3       +1
```

```
  2        1        3        6        4
 +0       +2       +1       +1       +1
```

```
  2        0        7        1        3
 +5       +5       +0       +5       +4
```

Practice and anything's possible!

```
  3        0        1
 +2       +0       +6
```

3

Addition

Name _____

Total Problems	**35**
Problems Correct	_____

$$\begin{array}{r} 3 \\ +7 \\ \hline \end{array} \qquad \begin{array}{r} 2 \\ +3 \\ \hline \end{array} \qquad \begin{array}{r} 1 \\ +4 \\ \hline \end{array}$$

$$\begin{array}{r} 2 \\ +4 \\ \hline \end{array} \quad \begin{array}{r} 5 \\ +4 \\ \hline \end{array} \quad \begin{array}{r} 6 \\ +2 \\ \hline \end{array} \quad \begin{array}{r} 3 \\ +5 \\ \hline \end{array} \quad \begin{array}{r} 10 \\ +0 \\ \hline \end{array} \quad \begin{array}{r} 2 \\ +8 \\ \hline \end{array} \quad \begin{array}{r} 3 \\ +3 \\ \hline \end{array}$$

$$\begin{array}{r} 0 \\ +1 \\ \hline \end{array} \quad \begin{array}{r} 6 \\ +4 \\ \hline \end{array} \quad \begin{array}{r} 5 \\ +0 \\ \hline \end{array} \quad \begin{array}{r} 5 \\ +3 \\ \hline \end{array} \quad \begin{array}{r} 7 \\ +3 \\ \hline \end{array} \quad \begin{array}{r} 1 \\ +8 \\ \hline \end{array} \quad \begin{array}{r} 2 \\ +2 \\ \hline \end{array}$$

$$\begin{array}{r} 7 \\ +2 \\ \hline \end{array} \quad \begin{array}{r} 4 \\ +4 \\ \hline \end{array} \quad \begin{array}{r} 1 \\ +2 \\ \hline \end{array} \quad \begin{array}{r} 9 \\ +1 \\ \hline \end{array} \quad \begin{array}{r} 3 \\ +6 \\ \hline \end{array} \quad \begin{array}{r} 6 \\ +1 \\ \hline \end{array} \quad \begin{array}{r} 5 \\ +2 \\ \hline \end{array}$$

$$\begin{array}{r} 8 \\ +2 \\ \hline \end{array} \quad \begin{array}{r} 4 \\ +3 \\ \hline \end{array} \quad \begin{array}{r} 2 \\ +7 \\ \hline \end{array} \quad \begin{array}{r} 0 \\ +3 \\ \hline \end{array} \quad \begin{array}{r} 2 \\ +5 \\ \hline \end{array} \quad \begin{array}{r} 0 \\ +9 \\ \hline \end{array} \quad \begin{array}{r} 5 \\ +1 \\ \hline \end{array}$$

Practice makes perfect!

$$\begin{array}{r} 6 \\ +3 \\ \hline \end{array} \quad \begin{array}{r} 2 \\ +6 \\ \hline \end{array} \quad \begin{array}{r} 5 \\ +5 \\ \hline \end{array} \quad \begin{array}{r} 8 \\ +0 \\ \hline \end{array}$$

Addition

Name _____

Total Problems	35
Problems Correct	_____

```
  5        0        8
 +3       +7       +1
____     ____     ____
```

```
  1        2        2        4        6        5        7
 +5       +5       +6       +2       +4       +0       +2
____     ____     ____     ____     ____     ____     ____
```

```
  4        9        2        2        6        4        5
 +1       +1       +8       +2       +3       +3       +1
____     ____     ____     ____     ____     ____     ____
```

```
  7        5        3        4        4        3        3
 +1       +4       +3       +5       +4       +1       +7
____     ____     ____     ____     ____     ____     ____
```

```
  4        3        2        3        1        1        6
 +6       +5       +7       +6       +7       +1       +1
____     ____     ____     ____     ____     ____     ____
```

Success ahoy! Just practice!

```
  6        1        3        5
 +2       +0       +2       +5
____     ____     ____     ____
```

Addition

Name _____

Total Problems	30
Problems Correct	_____

$3 + 6 =$

$2 + 0 =$

$6 + 2 =$ $2 + 6 =$ $6 + 3 =$

$1 + 3 =$ $0 + 1 =$ $1 + 6 =$

$5 + 1 =$ $5 + 3 =$ $2 + 1 =$

$9 + 0 =$ $4 + 1 =$ $4 + 3 =$

$5 + 2 =$ $4 + 5 =$ $5 + 5 =$

$7 + 2 =$ $1 + 3 =$ $8 + 2 =$

$3 + 4 =$ $0 + 4 =$ $6 + 4 =$

$2 + 8 =$ $4 + 2 =$ $3 + 2 =$

$6 + 0 =$ $4 + 6 =$ **Practice hard. You'll win!**

$7 + 3 =$ $3 + 7 =$

Addition

Name _____

Total Problems	25
Problems Correct	_____

```
  6        5
 +2       +4
```

```
  9        8        9        4        5
 +1       +3       +2       +3       +5
```

```
  3        5        7        5        8
 +5       +6       +3       +2       +1
```

```
  2        6       10        8        7
 +2       +3       +1       +2       +1
```

```
  7        3        0        6        4
 +2       +3       +7       +5       +7
```

Practice brings success!

```
  0        4        9
 +8       +6       +0
```

Addition

Name _____

Total Problems	**30**
Problems Correct	_____

$9 + 1 =$

$2 + 5 =$

$7 + 0 =$ $7 + 2 =$ $7 + 3 =$

$6 + 2 =$ $10 + 0 =$ $2 + 4 =$

$8 + 1 =$ $6 + 3 =$ $6 + 4 =$

$5 + 4 =$ $5 + 5 =$ $10 + 1 =$

$2 + 2 =$ $8 + 0 =$ $5 + 2 =$

$5 + 1 =$ $8 + 3 =$ $4 + 1 =$

$3 + 4 =$ $4 + 4 =$ $0 + 6 =$

$6 + 5 =$ $2 + 3 =$ $8 + 2 =$

Practice hard. You'll win!

$7 + 1 =$ $6 + 1 =$

$5 + 3 =$ $7 + 4 =$

Addition

Name _____

Total Problems	25
Problems Correct	_____

```
   3        7
 + 8      + 5
```

```
   5        6        7        8        6
 + 6      + 2      + 2      + 3      + 6
```

```
   8        5        7        6        9
 + 2      + 5      + 3      + 3      + 2
```

```
   3        5        6        3        4
 + 4      + 3      + 4      + 7      + 4
```

```
   7        9        3        8
 + 3      + 0      + 3      + 4
```

```
   9       10        5        9
 + 1      + 2      + 4      + 3
```

**Practice hard.
You'll win.**

9

Addition

Name _____

Total Problems	30
Problems Correct	_____

$7 + 0 =$

$8 + 2 =$

$7 + 5 =$ $5 + 5 =$ $5 + 4 =$

$9 + 3 =$ $8 + 4 =$ $3 + 9 =$

$10 + 1 =$ $2 + 5 =$ $7 + 4 =$

$5 + 4 =$ $11 + 1 =$ $7 + 5 =$

$9 + 2 =$ $7 + 3 =$ $5 + 5 =$

$6 + 3 =$ $8 + 0 =$ $6 + 6 =$

$5 + 6 =$ $10 + 2 =$ $8 + 3 =$

$9 + 1 =$ $3 + 3 =$ $7 + 2 =$

$4 + 4 =$ $9 + 0 =$ **Success ahoy! Just practice!**

$3 + 4 =$ $3 + 5 =$

Addition

Name _____

Total Problems	25
Problems Correct	_____

$$\begin{array}{r} 6 \\ +4 \\ \hline \end{array} \qquad \begin{array}{r} 8 \\ +5 \\ \hline \end{array}$$

$$\begin{array}{r} 9 \\ +2 \\ \hline \end{array} \qquad \begin{array}{r} 6 \\ +6 \\ \hline \end{array} \qquad \begin{array}{r} 11 \\ +2 \\ \hline \end{array} \qquad \begin{array}{r} 10 \\ +3 \\ \hline \end{array} \qquad \begin{array}{r} 6 \\ +3 \\ \hline \end{array}$$

$$\begin{array}{r} 3 \\ +4 \\ \hline \end{array} \qquad \begin{array}{r} 7 \\ +2 \\ \hline \end{array} \qquad \begin{array}{r} 9 \\ +4 \\ \hline \end{array} \qquad \begin{array}{r} 7 \\ +3 \\ \hline \end{array} \qquad \begin{array}{r} 8 \\ +4 \\ \hline \end{array}$$

$$\begin{array}{r} 7 \\ +4 \\ \hline \end{array} \qquad \begin{array}{r} 5 \\ +3 \\ \hline \end{array} \qquad \begin{array}{r} 4 \\ +4 \\ \hline \end{array} \qquad \begin{array}{r} 5 \\ +4 \\ \hline \end{array} \qquad \begin{array}{r} 7 \\ +6 \\ \hline \end{array}$$

$$\begin{array}{r} 10 \\ +2 \\ \hline \end{array} \qquad \begin{array}{r} 6 \\ +6 \\ \hline \end{array} \qquad \begin{array}{r} 8 \\ +2 \\ \hline \end{array} \qquad \begin{array}{r} 9 \\ +3 \\ \hline \end{array} \qquad \begin{array}{r} 6 \\ +5 \\ \hline \end{array}$$

$$\begin{array}{r} 7 \\ +6 \\ \hline \end{array} \qquad \begin{array}{r} 5 \\ +5 \\ \hline \end{array} \qquad \begin{array}{r} 8 \\ +3 \\ \hline \end{array}$$

Anything's possible with practice!

Addition

Name _____

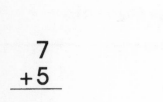

Total Problems	25
Problems Correct	_____

$$\begin{array}{r} 7 \\ +5 \\ \hline \end{array} \qquad \begin{array}{r} 9 \\ +5 \\ \hline \end{array}$$

$$\begin{array}{r} 6 \\ +5 \\ \hline \end{array} \quad \begin{array}{r} 7 \\ +7 \\ \hline \end{array} \quad \begin{array}{r} 8 \\ +5 \\ \hline \end{array} \quad \begin{array}{r} 6 \\ +6 \\ \hline \end{array} \quad \begin{array}{r} 9 \\ +4 \\ \hline \end{array}$$

$$\begin{array}{r} 9 \\ +2 \\ \hline \end{array} \quad \begin{array}{r} 6 \\ +4 \\ \hline \end{array} \quad \begin{array}{r} 8 \\ +6 \\ \hline \end{array} \quad \begin{array}{r} 7 \\ +4 \\ \hline \end{array} \quad \begin{array}{r} 9 \\ +1 \\ \hline \end{array}$$

$$\begin{array}{r} 8 \\ +3 \\ \hline \end{array} \quad \begin{array}{r} 10 \\ +4 \\ \hline \end{array} \quad \begin{array}{r} 3 \\ +7 \\ \hline \end{array} \quad \begin{array}{r} 5 \\ +5 \\ \hline \end{array} \quad \begin{array}{r} 6 \\ +8 \\ \hline \end{array}$$

$$\begin{array}{r} 9 \\ +3 \\ \hline \end{array} \quad \begin{array}{r} 5 \\ +2 \\ \hline \end{array} \quad \begin{array}{r} 7 \\ +6 \\ \hline \end{array} \quad \begin{array}{r} 5 \\ +9 \\ \hline \end{array} \quad \begin{array}{r} 4 \\ +5 \\ \hline \end{array}$$

$$\begin{array}{r} 6 \\ +3 \\ \hline \end{array} \quad \begin{array}{r} 4 \\ +9 \\ \hline \end{array} \quad \begin{array}{r} 3 \\ +4 \\ \hline \end{array}$$

**Practice hard.
You'll win!**

Addition

Name _____

Total Problems	30
Problems Correct	_____

```
   6          5
 + 7        + 5
```

```
   2          3          9          4          8          8
 + 9        + 8        + 5        + 7        + 4        + 3
```

```
   8          1          7          8          9          5
 + 5        + 9        + 5        + 6        + 3        + 6
```

```
   4          6          7          3          8          4
 + 9        + 5        + 3        + 9        + 5        + 8
```

```
   5          7          8          9          6          4
 + 8        + 7        + 2        + 4        + 8        + 6
```

Practice hard. You'll win.

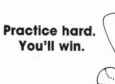

```
   6          5          5          7
 + 6        + 7        + 9        + 6
```

Addition

Name _____

Total Problems	30
Problems Correct	_____

```
   9        7
 +1      +6
```

```
   8        3        4        9        4        6
 +3      +7      +8      +2      +9      +5
```

```
  10        8        3        6        9        8
 +0      +5      +9      +7      +5      +2
```

```
   8        5        4        6        3        6
 +4      +6      +7      +4      +8      +8
```

```
   9        7        6        5        5        5
 +4      +7      +6      +7      +8      +9
```

```
   7        8        2        7
 +4      +6      +9      +5
```

Practice = Success!

Math IF8739   14   © 1990 Instructional Fair, Inc.

Addition

Name _____

Total Problems	__30__
Problems Correct	_____

3 + 7 =

5 + 6 =

2 + 9 =   6 + 7 =   8 + 4 =

6 + 6 =   9 + 2 =   4 + 7 =

4 + 6 =   4 + 9 =   1 + 9 =

3 + 8 =   5 + 8 =   7 + 6 =

6 + 8 =   2 + 8 =   7 + 5 =

7 + 3 =   7 + 7 =   9 + 3 =

7 + 4 =   4 + 8 =   6 + 5 =

9 + 4 =   5 + 9 =   8 + 6 =

3 + 9 =   9 + 5 =

Practice puts you on top!

8 + 5 =   8 + 3 =

Addition

Name _____

Total Problems	25
Problems Correct	_____

$$\begin{array}{r} 6 \\ +7 \\ \hline \end{array} \qquad \begin{array}{r} 8 \\ +7 \\ \hline \end{array}$$

$$\begin{array}{r} 8 \\ +5 \\ \hline \end{array} \qquad \begin{array}{r} 9 \\ +6 \\ \hline \end{array} \qquad \begin{array}{r} 7 \\ +4 \\ \hline \end{array} \qquad \begin{array}{r} 5 \\ +6 \\ \hline \end{array} \qquad \begin{array}{r} 9 \\ +5 \\ \hline \end{array}$$

$$\begin{array}{r} 6 \\ +3 \\ \hline \end{array} \qquad \begin{array}{r} 7 \\ +7 \\ \hline \end{array} \qquad \begin{array}{r} 8 \\ +6 \\ \hline \end{array} \qquad \begin{array}{r} 4 \\ +5 \\ \hline \end{array} \qquad \begin{array}{r} 8 \\ +2 \\ \hline \end{array}$$

$$\begin{array}{r} 7 \\ +8 \\ \hline \end{array} \qquad \begin{array}{r} 9 \\ +2 \\ \hline \end{array} \qquad \begin{array}{r} 7 \\ +5 \\ \hline \end{array} \qquad \begin{array}{r} 9 \\ +1 \\ \hline \end{array} \qquad \begin{array}{r} 8 \\ +4 \\ \hline \end{array}$$

$$\begin{array}{r} 6 \\ +6 \\ \hline \end{array} \qquad \begin{array}{r} 7 \\ +3 \\ \hline \end{array} \qquad \begin{array}{r} 7 \\ +6 \\ \hline \end{array} \qquad \begin{array}{r} 6 \\ +9 \\ \hline \end{array} \qquad \begin{array}{r} 9 \\ +3 \\ \hline \end{array}$$

Practice brings success!

$$\begin{array}{r} 9 \\ +4 \\ \hline \end{array} \qquad \begin{array}{r} 5 \\ +5 \\ \hline \end{array} \qquad \begin{array}{r} 8 \\ +3 \\ \hline \end{array}$$

Addition

Name _____

Total Problems	25
Problems Correct	_____

7
+8

8
+8

8
+5

9
+7

7
+6

6
+5

7
+7

5
+5

9
+3

6
+7

8
+3

7
+2

9
+6

6
+4

3
+9

7
+6

9
+4

7
+3

8
+4

6
+6

9
+5

6
+2

Practice! Practice! Practice!

7
+5

9
+2

8
+2

Addition

Name _____

Total Problems	25
Problems Correct	_____

```
  7        8
+ 8      + 9
```

```
  9        7        8        6        9
+ 6      + 7      + 5      + 5      + 3
```

```
  8        7        9        6        8
+ 4      + 6      + 8      + 6      + 2
```

```
  5        6        8        9        8
+ 6      + 4      + 8      + 2      + 7
```

```
  9        5        7        8        7
+ 4      + 5      + 5      + 6      + 4
```

```
  7        9        8
+ 3      + 1      + 6
```

Practice hard.   **You'll win!**

Addition

Name _____

Total Problems	**25**
Problems Correct	_____

```
  8        9
+ 8      + 4
```

```
  7        6        9        5        8
+ 3      + 6      + 8      + 5      + 6
```

```
  6        8        7        5        9
+ 7      + 5      + 7      + 6      + 3
```

```
  8        9        6        7        8
+ 4      + 7      + 4      + 6      + 3
```

```
  7        6        9        8        9
+ 4      + 3      + 9      + 2      + 6
```

```
  8        9        7
+ 7      + 5      + 5
```

Practice and anything's possible!

Math IF8739   19   © 1990 Instructional Fair, Inc.

Addition

Name _____

Total Problems	**30**
Problems Correct	_____

$$\begin{array}{r} 7 \\ +8 \\ \hline \end{array} \qquad \begin{array}{r} 9 \\ +5 \\ \hline \end{array}$$

$$\begin{array}{r} 8 \\ +8 \\ \hline \end{array} \quad \begin{array}{r} 9 \\ +9 \\ \hline \end{array} \quad \begin{array}{r} 5 \\ +8 \\ \hline \end{array} \quad \begin{array}{r} 7 \\ +3 \\ \hline \end{array} \quad \begin{array}{r} 9 \\ +7 \\ \hline \end{array} \quad \begin{array}{r} 8 \\ +7 \\ \hline \end{array}$$

$$\begin{array}{r} 6 \\ +9 \\ \hline \end{array} \quad \begin{array}{r} 5 \\ +7 \\ \hline \end{array} \quad \begin{array}{r} 9 \\ +6 \\ \hline \end{array} \quad \begin{array}{r} 2 \\ +9 \\ \hline \end{array} \quad \begin{array}{r} 8 \\ +9 \\ \hline \end{array} \quad \begin{array}{r} 7 \\ +7 \\ \hline \end{array}$$

$$\begin{array}{r} 9 \\ +8 \\ \hline \end{array} \quad \begin{array}{r} 9 \\ +1 \\ \hline \end{array} \quad \begin{array}{r} 4 \\ +8 \\ \hline \end{array} \quad \begin{array}{r} 9 \\ +9 \\ \hline \end{array} \quad \begin{array}{r} 6 \\ +9 \\ \hline \end{array} \quad \begin{array}{r} 6 \\ +4 \\ \hline \end{array}$$

$$\begin{array}{r} 5 \\ +9 \\ \hline \end{array} \quad \begin{array}{r} 8 \\ +9 \\ \hline \end{array} \quad \begin{array}{r} 6 \\ +8 \\ \hline \end{array} \quad \begin{array}{r} 3 \\ +9 \\ \hline \end{array} \quad \begin{array}{r} 4 \\ +9 \\ \hline \end{array} \quad \begin{array}{r} 7 \\ +6 \\ \hline \end{array}$$

$$\begin{array}{r} 6 \\ +5 \\ \hline \end{array} \quad \begin{array}{r} 3 \\ +8 \\ \hline \end{array} \quad \begin{array}{r} 7 \\ +9 \\ \hline \end{array} \quad \begin{array}{r} 8 \\ +6 \\ \hline \end{array}$$

Practice and anything's possible!

    © 1990 Instructional Fair, Inc.

Addition

Name _____

Total Problems	**30**
Problems Correct	_____

```
  9        6
 +4       +6
```

```
  8        2        9        5        7        8
 +7       +9       +9       +5       +6       +9
```

```
  7        6        9        8        8        7
 +4       +4       +8       +3       +8       +5
```

```
  5        6        7        9        5        6
 +8       +8       +9       +6       +9       +7
```

```
  5        7        6        8        2        7
 +6       +8       +9       +6       +8       +7
```

**Practice hard.
You'll win!**

```
  1        9        8        3
 +9       +7       +4       +9
```

Math IF8739   21   © 1990 Instructional Fair, Inc.

Addition

Name _____

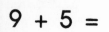

Total Problems	30
Problems Correct	_____

9 + 5 =

2 + 9 =

4 + 9 =   2 + 4 =   6 + 4 =

8 + 8 =   5 + 9 =   7 + 5 =

7 + 9 =   6 + 7 =   7 + 6 =

2 + 1 =   3 + 2 =   9 + 2 =

3 + 7 =   8 + 4 =   4 + 6 =

7 + 4 =   7 + 8 =   8 + 7 =

7 + 2 =   8 + 9 =   3 + 3 =

9 + 9 =   5 + 3 =   3 + 8 =

Anything's possible with practice!

8 + 3 =   9 + 3 =

6 + 8 =   0 + 4 =

Addition

Name _____

Total Problems	30
Problems Correct	_____

$7+9=$

$6+8=$

$9+7=$ $7+7=$ $2+9=$

$9+9=$ $8+9=$ $6+7=$

$8+6=$ $4+8=$ $8+2=$

$5+5=$ $5+6=$ $9+5=$

$8+7=$ $8+8=$ $7+8=$

$5+9=$ $5+7=$ $8+3=$

$9+8=$ $9+3=$ $8+5=$

$6+4=$ $9+6=$ $6+5=$

**Practice! Practice!
Practice!**

$8+8=$ $7+3=$

$6+9=$ $5+8=$

Missing Numbers

Name _____

Total Problems	25
Problems Correct	_____

$$2 + \square = 5$$ $$3 + \square = 3$$ $$1 + \square = 8$$

$$4 + \square = 8$$ $$4 + \square = 6$$ $$5 + \square = 8$$ $$3 + \square = 7$$ $$6 + \square = 9$$ $$2 + \square = 10$$

$$3 + \square = 9$$ $$8 + \square = 9$$ $$1 + \square = 1$$ $$0 + \square = 4$$ $$7 + \square = 9$$ $$2 + \square = 7$$

$$0 + \square = 7$$ $$5 + \square = 9$$ $$1 + \square = 2$$ $$3 + \square = 5$$ $$2 + \square = 9$$ $$1 + \square = 6$$

Practice and anything's possible!

$$6 + \square = 10$$ $$6 + \square = 8$$ $$7 + \square = 10$$ $$5 + \square = 7$$

Math IF8739

24

Missing Numbers

Name _____

Total Problems	25
Problems Correct	_____

9
+ ☐
—
17

3
+ ☐
—
12

7
+ ☐
—
13

5
+ ☐
—
14

7
+ ☐
—
12

9
+ ☐
—
15

7
+ ☐
—
16

7
+ ☐
—
11

8
+ ☐
—
16

8
+ ☐
—
12

7
+ ☐
—
14

8
+ ☐
—
17

6
+ ☐
—
12

3
+ ☐
—
11

6
+ ☐
—
13

9
+ ☐
—
13

9
+ ☐
—
14

6
+ ☐
—
15

9
+ ☐
—
18

8
+ ☐
—
14

7
+ ☐
—
15

9
+ ☐
—
11

6
+ ☐
—
14

6
+ ☐
—
11

8
+ ☐
—
13

Through practice you learn!

Missing Numbers

Name _____

Total Problems	__25__
Problems Correct	_____

$9 + \underline{\quad} = 11$

$1 + \underline{\quad} = 8$

$6 + \underline{\quad} = 13$ $4 + \underline{\quad} = 7$ $8 + \underline{\quad} = 13$

$7 + \underline{\quad} = 15$ $7 + \underline{\quad} = 9$ $0 + \underline{\quad} = 7$

$8 + \underline{\quad} = 12$ $8 + \underline{\quad} = 17$ $5 + \underline{\quad} = 11$

$5 + \underline{\quad} = 10$ $6 + \underline{\quad} = 12$ $9 + \underline{\quad} = 14$

$4 + \underline{\quad} = 11$ $3 + \underline{\quad} = 10$ $8 + \underline{\quad} = 15$

$8 + \underline{\quad} = 14$ $9 + \underline{\quad} = 13$ $5 + \underline{\quad} = 9$

$9 + \underline{\quad} = 12$ $2 + \underline{\quad} = 10$ $9 + \underline{\quad} = 16$

$3 + \underline{\quad} = 9$

$0 + \underline{\quad} = 8$

With practice, you can do it!

Math IF8739

Addition

Name _____

Total Problems	25
Problems Correct	_____

```
  2        3
  1        0
+ 2      + 1
```

```
  1        2        0        2        1
  1        1        2        0        3
+ 1      + 3      + 2      + 1      + 0
```

```
  3        2        1        2        5
  1        1        2        1        1
+ 2      + 0      + 1      + 0      + 0
```

```
  4        2        2        3        0
  0        3        0        1        5
+ 1      + 1      + 4      + 0      + 1
```

```
  2        5        3        4        0
  1        0        0        1        3
+ 2      + 1      + 2      + 1      + 1
```

```
  2        3        0
  1        2        4
+ 0      + 1      + 1
```

Practice = Success!

Addition

Name _____

Total Problems	30
Problems Correct	_____

$5 + 0 + 1 =$

$1 + 2 + 3 =$

$2 + 0 + 3 =$ $2 + 1 + 1 =$ $4 + 0 + 1 =$

$1 + 1 + 1 =$ $0 + 2 + 3 =$ $3 + 1 + 2 =$

$1 + 2 + 1 =$ $0 + 3 + 1 =$ $1 + 0 + 1 =$

$4 + 0 + 2 =$ $2 + 2 + 2 =$ $3 + 1 + 1 =$

$3 + 0 + 1 =$ $1 + 1 + 3 =$ $0 + 2 + 4 =$

$2 + 1 + 0 =$ $3 + 1 + 0 =$ $3 + 0 + 2 =$

$2 + 0 + 2 =$ $1 + 2 + 2 =$ $4 + 2 + 0 =$

$2 + 1 + 2 =$ $2 + 0 + 1 =$ $1 + 1 + 3 =$

Practice hard. You'll win!

$1 + 1 + 2 =$ $4 + 1 + 1 =$

$1 + 3 + 2 =$ $0 + 4 + 1 =$

Addition

Name _____

Total Problems	25
Problems Correct	_____

```
   3          5
   0          1
 + 4        + 2
```

```
   6          4          2          5          4
   0          2          3          1          3
 + 4        + 2        + 1        + 2        + 2
```

```
   2          3          8          3          7
   5          0          0          3          1
 + 2        + 4        + 1        + 4        + 2
```

```
   5          2          6          3          8
   2          2          2          2          0
 + 1        + 2        + 1        + 3        + 1
```

```
   2          6          2          7          5
   2          1          3          2          1
 + 4        + 0        + 4        + 1        + 2
```

Practice! Practice! Practice!

```
   6          0          3
   3          4          3
 + 1        + 2        + 3
```

Addition

Name _____

Total Problems	**30**
Problems Correct	_____

$7 + 2 + 1 =$

$3 + 0 + 4 =$

$5 + 2 + 3 =$ $3 + 3 + 2 =$ $5 + 3 + 1 =$

$6 + 1 + 2 =$ $5 + 4 + 1 =$ $2 + 3 + 2 =$

$2 + 4 + 1 =$ $6 + 2 + 0 =$ $4 + 2 + 3 =$

$3 + 3 + 3 =$ $4 + 0 + 2 =$ $8 + 1 + 0 =$

$6 + 0 + 1 =$ $6 + 1 + 0 =$ $2 + 0 + 3 =$

$4 + 2 + 2 =$ $2 + 2 + 2 =$ $6 + 3 + 1 =$

$5 + 2 + 1 =$ $3 + 4 + 1 =$ $3 + 0 + 3 =$

$7 + 0 + 2 =$ $1 + 2 + 1 =$ $5 + 1 + 1 =$

Success ahoy! Just practice!

$2 + 2 + 6 =$ $6 + 3 + 1 =$

$5 + 1 + 3 =$ $7 + 0 + 1 =$

Addition

Name _____

Total Problems	25
Problems Correct	_____

```
   4        3        1
   1        6        5
  +9       +9       +6
  ___      ___      ___
```

```
   2        2        6        6        5        9
   8        4        2        0        4        0
  +4       +5       +4       +5       +7       +4
  ___      ___      ___      ___      ___      ___
```

```
   3        8        3        5        7        2
   4        1        2        2        0        3
  +7       +7       +9       +6       +7       +6
  ___      ___      ___      ___      ___      ___
```

```
   1        4        2        3        9        4
   6        3        2        5        0        1
  +3       +8       +9       +7       +8       +6
  ___      ___      ___      ___      ___      ___
```

Practice! Practice! Practice!

```
   5        4        2        2
   2        4        3        6
  +8       +8       +5       +9
  ___      ___      ___      ___
```

Addition

Name ______________________

Total Problems	**25**
Problems Correct	______

2	1	5
3	0	2
+6	+8	+6

4	8	6	2	3	2
3	0	3	3	3	2
+5	+3	+5	+9	+9	+6

5	7	1	4	4	3
4	2	3	2	5	5
+8	+8	+8	+8	+7	+7

6	2	6	4	5	5
4	4	2	4	1	5
+0	+5	+6	+8	+7	+1

7	8	9	1
1	1	1	5
+7	+9	+5	+6

Practice = Success!

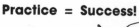

Addition

Name _____

Total Problems ____25____

Problems Correct _____

```
  55        47
+ 32      + 21
```

```
  37        65        44        62        14
+ 51      + 34      + 32      + 34      + 42
```

```
  75        36        16        25        52
+ 24      + 41      + 60      + 53      + 42
```

```
  23        43        28        37        61
+ 14      + 25      + 51      + 30      + 26
```

```
  42        30        37        55        46
+ 51      + 48      + 22      + 22      + 30
```

```
  60        15        70
+ 18      + 13      + 11
```

**Practice hard.
You'll win.**

Addition

Name _____

Total Problems	25
Problems Correct	_____

$$61 + 27$$ $$24 + 24$$

$$14 + 24$$ $$23 + 52$$ $$40 + 40$$ $$60 + 20$$ $$46 + 53$$

$$24 + 35$$ $$35 + 34$$ $$30 + 40$$ $$21 + 52$$ $$70 + 18$$

$$45 + 30$$ $$34 + 12$$ $$72 + 14$$ $$35 + 13$$ $$24 + 43$$

$$25 + 61$$ $$42 + 17$$ $$53 + 23$$ $$10 + 50$$ $$24 + 44$$

$$52 + 20$$ $$33 + 14$$ $$54 + 13$$

With practice, you can do it!

Addition

Name _____

Total Problems	25
Problems Correct	_____

$$95 + 33$$ $$94 + 93$$

$$71 + 71$$ $$27 + 82$$ $$94 + 64$$ $$71 + 66$$ $$85 + 91$$

$$74 + 95$$ $$33 + 85$$ $$44 + 92$$ $$82 + 71$$ $$52 + 85$$

$$93 + 26$$ $$60 + 85$$ $$53 + 72$$ $$41 + 75$$ $$32 + 72$$

$$95 + 44$$ $$52 + 56$$ $$80 + 60$$ $$92 + 54$$ $$83 + 84$$

$$97 + 81$$ $$43 + 83$$ $$74 + 80$$

With practice, you can do it!

Addition

Name _____

Total Problems	25
Problems Correct	_____

```
  47        30
+ 51      + 20
```

```
  64        32        56        43        15
+ 32      + 27      + 20      + 25      + 10
```

```
  54        24        35        11        12
+ 13      + 15      + 42      + 62      + 12
```

```
  23        20        16        12        51
+ 62      + 71      + 42      + 15      + 25
```

```
  21        31        42        70        27
+ 16      + 13      + 20      + 10      + 32
```

```
  76        55        52
+ 23      + 14      + 33
```

Through practice you learn!

Addition

Name _____

Total Problems	25
Problems Correct	_____

```
   25        72
 + 32      + 17
```

```
   81        62        11        44        42
 + 10      + 36      + 18      + 23      + 21
```

```
   61        35        10        19        23
 + 26      + 43      + 60      + 20      + 53
```

```
   14        45        33        28        60
 + 41      + 14      + 42      + 61      + 34
```

```
   37        41        12        14        24
 + 22      + 41      + 21      + 54      + 72
```

Practice and anything's possible!

```
   15        63        21
 + 11      + 21      + 25
```

Addition

Name _____

Total Problems	25
Problems Correct	_____

```
  72        17
+ 22      + 37
```

```
  16        49        56        32        20
+ 15      + 11      + 19      + 47      + 16
```

```
  36        57        24        68        39
+ 17      + 39      + 44      + 25      + 39
```

```
  49        55        29        48        23
+ 24      + 33      + 28      + 17      + 14
```

```
  36        12        28        21        19
+ 45      + 58      + 24      + 22      + 67
```

Practice brings success!

```
  47        27        52
+ 35      + 18      + 43
```

Addition

Name _____

Total Problems	25
Problems Correct	_____

```
  15          29
+ 16        + 33
```

```
  38          56          17          19          40
+ 28        + 26        + 60        + 16        + 17
```

```
  35          31          36          45          13
+ 15        + 58        + 18        + 39        + 28
```

```
  63          26          49          22          30
+ 23        + 27        + 39        + 43        + 40
```

```
  53          16          81          38          42
+ 46        + 58        + 12        + 29        + 38
```

Anything's possible with practice!

```
  77          19          54
+ 13        + 18        + 25
```

39

Addition

Name _____

Total Problems	25
Problems Correct	_____

```
  18        77
+ 26      + 16
```

```
  49        34        67        17        56
+ 12      + 29      + 13      + 18      + 36
```

```
  22        75        28        46        37
+ 49      + 19      + 39      + 24      + 19
```

```
  28        28        19        65        39
+ 25      + 44      + 19      + 16      + 45
```

```
  61        23        46        29        18
+ 29      + 59      + 38      + 16      + 78
```

```
  38        42        35
+ 17      + 48      + 26
```

Practice makes perfect!

Addition

Name _____

Total Problems	**25**
Problems Correct	_____

```
  38          47
+ 12        + 15
```

```
  49          27          16          66          18
+ 28        + 36        + 45        + 29        + 56
```

```
  28          49          67          39          38
+ 15        + 38        + 27        + 17        + 47
```

```
  57          26          17          34          18
+ 39        + 26        + 24        + 36        + 19
```

```
  35          58          23          29          19
+ 29        + 14        + 27        + 29        + 74
```

Practice = Success!

```
  66          38          59
+ 15        + 13        + 19
```

Addition

Name _____

Total Problems	25
Problems Correct	_____

```
  55        13
+ 37      + 28
```

```
  44        48        37        78        15
+ 38      + 27      + 17      + 19      + 28
```

```
  66        42        21        65        38
+ 27      + 29      + 39      + 26      + 36
```

```
  22        27        26        29        18
+ 18      + 19      + 59      + 23      + 18
```

```
  39        16        67        14        24
+ 38      + 16      + 18      + 49      + 56
```

```
  34        49        45
+ 37      + 39      + 19
```

Practice puts you on top!

Addition

Name _____

Total Problems	25
Problems Correct	_____

```
  522        124
+ 344      +  50
_____      _____
```

```
   26         53        608        171        200
 + 60       + 26      + 201      + 16      + 300
 ____       ____      _____      ____      _____
```

```
  376        701         43        330        141
+ 103      + 217       + 20      + 150      + 121
_____      _____       ____      _____      _____
```

```
  800        164        135        918         70
 + 53       + 14      + 221      + 60       + 20
 ____       ____      _____      ____       ____
```

```
   12        640        252        461        445
 + 33       + 35       + 32      + 327       + 53
 ____       ____       ____      _____       ____
```

```
  112        251        232
+ 205      + 740      + 344
_____      _____      _____
```

Practice! Practice! Practice!

Addition

Name _____

Total Problems	25
Problems Correct	_____

```
  284        534
+ 513      + 225
```

```
  625        130        472        242        120
+ 243      + 160      + 227      + 314      + 345
```

```
  391        423        112        362        513
+ 408      + 152      + 203      + 322      + 373
```

```
  303        421        661        231        710
+ 104      + 221      + 235      + 212      + 213
```

```
  446        212        531        320        255
+ 152      + 162      + 432      + 131      + 432
```

Practice! Practice! Practice!

```
  234        300        191
+ 304      + 200      + 101
```

Subtraction

Name _____

Total Problems	25
Problems Correct	_____

```
  4        6
 -2       -5
____      ____
```

```
  5        4        3        5        1
 -1       -4       -1       -0       -1
____      ____     ____     ____     ____
```

```
  3        5        6        4        6
 -2       -4       -3       -3       -0
____      ____     ____     ____     ____
```

```
  4        2        6        3        6
 -1       -0       -5       -3       -1
____      ____     ____     ____     ____
```

```
  6        6        1        5        2
 -4       -6       -0       -3       -2
____      ____     ____     ____     ____
```

Practice brings success!

```
  5        4        0
 -2       -0       -0
____      ____     ____
```

Math IF8739   45   © 1990 Instructional Fair, Inc.

Subtraction

Name _____

Total Problems	30
Problems Correct	_____

$2 - 0 =$

$5 - 2 =$

$4 - 0 =$ $4 - 1 =$ $6 - 3 =$

$0 - 0 =$ $6 - 0 =$ $3 - 2 =$

$5 - 3 =$ $4 - 3 =$ $5 - 5 =$

$2 - 2 =$ $6 - 3 =$ $6 - 2 =$

$1 - 0 =$ $5 - 4 =$ $5 - 1 =$

$6 - 4 =$ $4 - 4 =$ $2 - 0 =$

$6 - 6 =$ $5 - 0 =$ $3 - 1 =$

$6 - 5 =$ $1 - 1 =$ $6 - 2 =$

With practice, you can do it!

$3 - 3 =$ $3 - 0 =$

$6 - 1 =$ $5 - 2 =$

Subtraction

Name _____

Total Problems	25
Problems Correct	_____

$$\begin{array}{r} 6 \\ -3 \\ \hline \end{array} \qquad \begin{array}{r} 5 \\ -2 \\ \hline \end{array}$$

$$\begin{array}{r} 4 \\ -4 \\ \hline \end{array} \qquad \begin{array}{r} 7 \\ -3 \\ \hline \end{array} \qquad \begin{array}{r} 5 \\ -4 \\ \hline \end{array} \qquad \begin{array}{r} 7 \\ -5 \\ \hline \end{array} \qquad \begin{array}{r} 4 \\ -2 \\ \hline \end{array}$$

$$\begin{array}{r} 7 \\ -2 \\ \hline \end{array} \qquad \begin{array}{r} 3 \\ -0 \\ \hline \end{array} \qquad \begin{array}{r} 4 \\ -3 \\ \hline \end{array} \qquad \begin{array}{r} 5 \\ -0 \\ \hline \end{array} \qquad \begin{array}{r} 6 \\ -4 \\ \hline \end{array}$$

$$\begin{array}{r} 3 \\ -2 \\ \hline \end{array} \qquad \begin{array}{r} 6 \\ -2 \\ \hline \end{array} \qquad \begin{array}{r} 2 \\ -1 \\ \hline \end{array} \qquad \begin{array}{r} 3 \\ -3 \\ \hline \end{array} \qquad \begin{array}{r} 6 \\ -5 \\ \hline \end{array}$$

$$\begin{array}{r} 7 \\ -1 \\ \hline \end{array} \qquad \begin{array}{r} 7 \\ -6 \\ \hline \end{array} \qquad \begin{array}{r} 6 \\ -1 \\ \hline \end{array} \qquad \begin{array}{r} 0 \\ -0 \\ \hline \end{array} \qquad \begin{array}{r} 7 \\ -4 \\ \hline \end{array}$$

With practice, you can do it!

$$\begin{array}{r} 7 \\ -0 \\ \hline \end{array} \qquad \begin{array}{r} 4 \\ -1 \\ \hline \end{array} \qquad \begin{array}{r} 5 \\ -3 \\ \hline \end{array}$$

47

Subtraction

Name _____

Total Problems	30
Problems Correct	_____

4 – 0 =

5 – 2 =

6 – 3 =   6 – 4 =   7 – 3 =

4 – 2 =   3 – 3 =   1 – 1 =

7 – 0 =   6 – 4 =   7 – 5 =

5 – 1 =   3 – 2 =   4 – 1 =

7 – 1 =   2 – 2 =   5 – 5 =

5 – 0 =   6 – 2 =   3 – 1 =

4 – 4 =   0 – 0 =   7 – 6 =

7 – 2 =   6 – 5 =   5 – 3 =

3 – 0 =   7 – 3 =

Practice = Success!

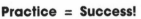

4 – 3 =   2 – 0 =

Subtraction

Name _____

Total Problems	**25**
Problems Correct	_____

$$\begin{array}{r} 5 \\ -2 \\ \hline \end{array} \qquad \begin{array}{r} 7 \\ -7 \\ \hline \end{array}$$

$$\begin{array}{r} 8 \\ -3 \\ \hline \end{array} \qquad \begin{array}{r} 6 \\ -2 \\ \hline \end{array} \qquad \begin{array}{r} 7 \\ -4 \\ \hline \end{array} \qquad \begin{array}{r} 6 \\ -6 \\ \hline \end{array} \qquad \begin{array}{r} 8 \\ -4 \\ \hline \end{array}$$

$$\begin{array}{r} 6 \\ -3 \\ \hline \end{array} \qquad \begin{array}{r} 8 \\ -6 \\ \hline \end{array} \qquad \begin{array}{r} 5 \\ -5 \\ \hline \end{array} \qquad \begin{array}{r} 8 \\ -0 \\ \hline \end{array} \qquad \begin{array}{r} 7 \\ -1 \\ \hline \end{array}$$

$$\begin{array}{r} 6 \\ -4 \\ \hline \end{array} \qquad \begin{array}{r} 7 \\ -2 \\ \hline \end{array} \qquad \begin{array}{r} 6 \\ -5 \\ \hline \end{array} \qquad \begin{array}{r} 8 \\ -1 \\ \hline \end{array} \qquad \begin{array}{r} 5 \\ -4 \\ \hline \end{array}$$

$$\begin{array}{r} 4 \\ -2 \\ \hline \end{array} \qquad \begin{array}{r} 8 \\ -5 \\ \hline \end{array} \qquad \begin{array}{r} 5 \\ -3 \\ \hline \end{array} \qquad \begin{array}{r} 8 \\ -7 \\ \hline \end{array} \qquad \begin{array}{r} 7 \\ -3 \\ \hline \end{array}$$

$$\begin{array}{r} 7 \\ -6 \\ \hline \end{array} \qquad \begin{array}{r} 8 \\ -2 \\ \hline \end{array} \qquad \begin{array}{r} 6 \\ -0 \\ \hline \end{array}$$

Practice! Practice! Practice!

Subtraction

Name _____

Total Problems	30
Problems Correct	_____

7 – 6 =

6 – 4 =

7 – 2 =   6 – 6 =   2 – 2 =

5 – 0 =   8 – 2 =   5 – 2 =

8 – 1 =   6 – 3 =   7 – 7 =

5 – 4 =   7 – 4 =   8 – 5 =

3 – 3 =   6 – 4 =   7 – 5 =

4 – 2 =   7 – 3 =   5 – 1 =

7 – 0 =   8 – 0 =   4 – 4 =

5 – 3 =   5 – 5 =   6 – 5 =

Practice and anything's possible!

8 – 7 =   7 – 1 =

7 – 3 =   8 – 3 =

Subtraction

Name _____

Total Problems	25
Problems Correct	_____

```
  8        9
 -6       -3
```

```
  7        8        9        5        8
 -5       -8       -4       -3       -2
```

```
  9        7        8        9        7
 -0       -2       -3       -6       -4
```

```
  9        5        9        7        6
 -5       -4       -1       -3       -2
```

```
  8        6        9        7        8
 -1       -5       -2       -1       -4
```

Practice! Practice! Practice!

```
  9        8        7
 -9       -5       -6
```

51

Subtraction

Name _____

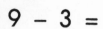

9 – 3 =

7 – 2 =

9 – 0 =   5 – 4 =   6 – 6 =

8 – 3 =   9 – 5 =   8 – 0 =

9 – 6 =   7 – 3 =   7 – 6 =

7 – 4 =   9 – 1 =   8 – 4 =

8 – 2 =   6 – 2 =   7 – 1 =

5 – 3 =   4 – 4 =   6 – 3 =

9 – 4 =   7 – 0 =   7 – 7 =

8 – 8 =   8 – 1 =   8 – 6 =

Practice and anything's possible!

7 – 5 =   6 – 5 =

9 – 9 =   9 – 2 =

Subtraction

Name _____

Total Problems	25
Problems Correct	_____

```
  7        10
- 5       - 3
____      ____
```

```
  8        10         7         9         8
- 6       - 4       - 3       - 6       - 7
____      ____      ____      ____      ____
```

```
 10         9         8        10         9
- 5       - 3       - 7       - 1       - 6
____      ____      ____      ____      ____
```

```
  8         9        10         7         8
- 2       - 5       - 0       - 6       - 4
____      ____      ____      ____      ____
```

```
  7        10         9        10         7
- 2       - 4       - 4       -10       - 4
____      ____      ____      ____      ____
```

Anything's possible with practice!

```
 10         6         8
- 2       - 2       - 5
____      ____      ____
```

Subtraction

Name _____

Total Problems	30
Problems Correct	_____

9 – 6 =

8 – 2 =

7 – 5 =	8 – 7 =	9 – 2 =
10 – 3 =	6 – 0 =	8 – 3 =
7 – 2 =	9 – 1 =	9 – 4 =
10 – 0 =	10 – 4 =	10 – 2 =
7 – 6 =	8 – 6 =	7 – 4 =
8 – 4 =	0 – 0 =	6 – 2 =
10 – 5 =	9 – 0 =	10 – 10 =
9 – 3 =	10 – 0 =	8 – 5 =

Practice brings success!

8 – 1 =	9 – 5 =	
10 – 1 =	8 – 2 =	

Math IF8739

Subtraction

Name _____

Total Problems	35
Problems Correct	_____

$$\begin{array}{r} 10 \\ -3 \\ \hline \end{array}$$ $$\begin{array}{r} 5 \\ -2 \\ \hline \end{array}$$ $$\begin{array}{r} 5 \\ -1 \\ \hline \end{array}$$

$$\begin{array}{r} 6 \\ -2 \\ \hline \end{array}$$ $$\begin{array}{r} 9 \\ -5 \\ \hline \end{array}$$ $$\begin{array}{r} 8 \\ -6 \\ \hline \end{array}$$ $$\begin{array}{r} 8 \\ -3 \\ \hline \end{array}$$ $$\begin{array}{r} 10 \\ -0 \\ \hline \end{array}$$ $$\begin{array}{r} 10 \\ -2 \\ \hline \end{array}$$ $$\begin{array}{r} 6 \\ -3 \\ \hline \end{array}$$

$$\begin{array}{r} 1 \\ -0 \\ \hline \end{array}$$ $$\begin{array}{r} 10 \\ -6 \\ \hline \end{array}$$ $$\begin{array}{r} 8 \\ -5 \\ \hline \end{array}$$ $$\begin{array}{r} 10 \\ -7 \\ \hline \end{array}$$ $$\begin{array}{r} 9 \\ -1 \\ \hline \end{array}$$ $$\begin{array}{r} 4 \\ -2 \\ \hline \end{array}$$ $$\begin{array}{r} 9 \\ -7 \\ \hline \end{array}$$

$$\begin{array}{r} 8 \\ -4 \\ \hline \end{array}$$ $$\begin{array}{r} 3 \\ -1 \\ \hline \end{array}$$ $$\begin{array}{r} 10 \\ -9 \\ \hline \end{array}$$ $$\begin{array}{r} 9 \\ -3 \\ \hline \end{array}$$ $$\begin{array}{r} 7 \\ -6 \\ \hline \end{array}$$ $$\begin{array}{r} 7 \\ -5 \\ \hline \end{array}$$ $$\begin{array}{r} 10 \\ -8 \\ \hline \end{array}$$

$$\begin{array}{r} 7 \\ -4 \\ \hline \end{array}$$ $$\begin{array}{r} 9 \\ -2 \\ \hline \end{array}$$ $$\begin{array}{r} 3 \\ -0 \\ \hline \end{array}$$ $$\begin{array}{r} 1 \\ -1 \\ \hline \end{array}$$ $$\begin{array}{r} 7 \\ -2 \\ \hline \end{array}$$ $$\begin{array}{r} 9 \\ -0 \\ \hline \end{array}$$ $$\begin{array}{r} 6 \\ -5 \\ \hline \end{array}$$

$$\begin{array}{r} 9 \\ -6 \\ \hline \end{array}$$ $$\begin{array}{r} 2 \\ -1 \\ \hline \end{array}$$ $$\begin{array}{r} 4 \\ -3 \\ \hline \end{array}$$ $$\begin{array}{r} 6 \\ -1 \\ \hline \end{array}$$

Practice hard. You'll win.

55

Subtraction

Name _____

Total Problems	**35**
Problems Correct	_____

$10 - 8 =$

$4 - 1 =$ $\qquad$ $7 - 6 =$ $\qquad$ $10 - 5 =$

$5 - 0 =$ $\qquad$ $6 - 4 =$ $\qquad$ $8 - 0 =$

$10 - 6 =$ $\qquad$ $8 - 2 =$ $\qquad$ $5 - 2 =$

$6 - 1 =$ $\qquad$ $7 - 5 =$ $\qquad$ $3 - 3 =$

$10 - 4 =$ $\qquad$ $4 - 2 =$ $\qquad$ $9 - 4 =$

$9 - 6 =$ $\qquad$ $5 - 3 =$ $\qquad$ $10 - 10 =$

$8 - 3 =$ $\qquad$ $8 - 1 =$ $\qquad$ $6 - 2 =$

$9 - 3 =$ $\qquad$ $6 - 3 =$ $\qquad$ $1 - 1 =$

$8 - 8 =$ $\qquad$ $2 - 2 =$ $\qquad$ $10 - 7 =$

$10 - 1 =$ $\qquad$ $9 - 5 =$ $\qquad$ $7 - 3 =$

$1 - 0 =$ $\qquad$ $6 - 6 =$ $\qquad$ **Practice brings success!**

$3 - 2 =$ $\qquad$ $7 - 2 =$

Subtraction

Name _____

Total Problems	35
Problems Correct	_____

```
  10        1        9
 - 9      - 1      - 2
 ----     ----     ----
```

```
   3        5        9        6        2       10        6
 - 1      - 4      - 9      - 5      - 2      - 8      - 6
 ----     ----     ----     ----     ----     ----     ----
```

```
   1       10        3        8        4        5        9
 - 0      - 7      - 2      - 7      - 2      - 3      - 0
 ----     ----     ----     ----     ----     ----     ----
```

```
   9        6        8        3       10        5       10
 - 8      - 4      - 6      - 3      - 1      - 2      - 5
 ----     ----     ----     ----     ----     ----     ----
```

```
   4        6       10        5        8        6        9
 - 3      - 2      - 2      - 1      - 5      - 3      - 7
 ----     ----     ----     ----     ----     ----     ----
```

```
   9        2        8       10
 - 1      - 1      - 4      - 3
 ----     ----     ----     ----
```

Practice makes perfect!

57

Subtraction

Name _____

Total Problems	25
Problems Correct	_____

$$\begin{array}{r} 10 \\ -2 \\ \hline \end{array} \qquad \begin{array}{r} 9 \\ -3 \\ \hline \end{array}$$

$$\begin{array}{r} 11 \\ -6 \\ \hline \end{array} \quad \begin{array}{r} 8 \\ -7 \\ \hline \end{array} \quad \begin{array}{r} 7 \\ -6 \\ \hline \end{array} \quad \begin{array}{r} 10 \\ -4 \\ \hline \end{array} \quad \begin{array}{r} 11 \\ -3 \\ \hline \end{array}$$

$$\begin{array}{r} 9 \\ -8 \\ \hline \end{array} \quad \begin{array}{r} 8 \\ -6 \\ \hline \end{array} \quad \begin{array}{r} 11 \\ -1 \\ \hline \end{array} \quad \begin{array}{r} 9 \\ -2 \\ \hline \end{array} \quad \begin{array}{r} 10 \\ -5 \\ \hline \end{array}$$

$$\begin{array}{r} 11 \\ -10 \\ \hline \end{array} \quad \begin{array}{r} 10 \\ -8 \\ \hline \end{array} \quad \begin{array}{r} 11 \\ -9 \\ \hline \end{array} \quad \begin{array}{r} 9 \\ -6 \\ \hline \end{array} \quad \begin{array}{r} 11 \\ -5 \\ \hline \end{array}$$

$$\begin{array}{r} 11 \\ -4 \\ \hline \end{array} \quad \begin{array}{r} 10 \\ -6 \\ \hline \end{array} \quad \begin{array}{r} 10 \\ -7 \\ \hline \end{array} \quad \begin{array}{r} 7 \\ -5 \\ \hline \end{array} \quad \begin{array}{r} 9 \\ -5 \\ \hline \end{array}$$

$$\begin{array}{r} 9 \\ -0 \\ \hline \end{array} \quad \begin{array}{r} 8 \\ -5 \\ \hline \end{array} \quad \begin{array}{r} 11 \\ -2 \\ \hline \end{array}$$

With practice, you can do it!

58

Subtraction

Name _____

Total Problems	__30__
Problems Correct	_____

$11-5=$

$9-5=$

$11-7=$ $10-8=$ $11-3=$

$7-5=$ $11-10=$ $10-7=$

$10-6=$ $10-5=$ $7-6=$

$11-4=$ $9-2=$ $7-2=$

$9-0=$ $11-1=$ $8-7=$

$8-5=$ $8-6=$ $5-2=$

$11-2=$ $9-8=$ $11-6=$

$9-6=$ $11-3=$ $8-5=$

$11-9=$ $10-7=$

$10-8=$ $7-6=$

Practice puts you on top!

Subtraction

Name _____

Total Problems	**25**
Problems Correct	_____

```
  11        12
 - 3       - 4
```

```
   9        11        12        11         9
 - 6       - 5       - 9       - 8       - 3
```

```
  12        11         7        10        12
 - 8       - 6       - 5       - 6       - 3
```

```
  11        12         9        10         8
 - 4       - 7       - 5       - 4       - 4
```

```
  12        10        11        12        10
 - 2       - 3       - 3       - 6       - 5
```

```
  10        12        11
 - 7       - 5       - 2
```

Practice = Success!

Math IF8739   60   © 1990 Instructional Fair, Inc.

Subtraction

Name _____

Total Problems	**30**
Problems Correct	_____

11 – 7 =

10 – 2 =

11 – 4 =   12 – 1 =   11 – 5 =

12 – 2 =   10 – 3 =   10 – 1 =

8 – 4 =   12 – 9 =   12 – 4 =

10 – 7 =   11 – 8 =   10 – 6 =

8 – 5 =   12 – 5 =   8 – 3 =

12 – 3 =   10 – 4 =   11 – 9 =

7 – 6 =   11 – 6 =   12 – 6 =

11 – 3 =   9 – 3 =   9 – 2 =

9 – 8 =   12 – 8 =

12 – 10 =   8 – 6 =

**Anything's possible
with practice!**

Subtraction

Name _____

Total Problems	25
Problems Correct	_____

```
 11        13
- 8       - 2
____      ____
```

```
 10        12        10        12        13
- 3       - 9       - 5       - 5       - 5
____      ____      ____      ____      ____
```

```
 11        13        10        11        12
- 7       - 4       - 6       - 6       - 4
____      ____      ____      ____      ____
```

```
 10        12        13        12        13
- 9       - 6       - 8       - 7       - 7
____      ____      ____      ____      ____
```

```
 12        13        10        12        11
- 3       - 6       - 4       - 8       - 5
____      ____      ____      ____      ____
```

```
 11        13        12
- 9       - 9       - 7
____      ____      ____
```

**Practice puts you
on top!**

62

Subtraction

Name _____

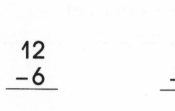

Total Problems	25
Problems Correct	_____

```
  12        14
 - 6       - 9
_____     _____
```

```
  10        14        11        13        12
 - 6       - 5       - 7       - 8       - 5
_____     _____     _____     _____     _____
```

```
  11        13        12        14        11
 - 2       - 5       - 9       - 6       - 8
_____     _____     _____     _____     _____
```

```
  13        12        13        14        14
 - 6       - 8       - 7       - 4       - 2
_____     _____     _____     _____     _____
```

```
  10        12        10        14        13
 - 4       - 7       - 8       - 7       - 9
_____     _____     _____     _____     _____
```

```
  11        14        13
 - 9       - 8       - 4
_____     _____     _____
```

Practice = Success!

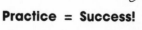

Subtraction

Name _____

Total Problems	30
Problems Correct	_____

```
  13        11
 - 4       - 3
-----      -----
```

```
  12        14        10        13         8        11
 - 4       - 5       - 2       - 5       - 3       - 8
-----      -----     -----     -----     -----     -----
```

```
  14        12        11         7        10        12
 - 9       - 3       - 7       - 2       - 9       - 5
-----      -----     -----     -----     -----     -----
```

```
  11        13        14        10        13        11
 - 9       - 6       - 8       - 6       - 7       - 6
-----      -----     -----     -----     -----     -----
```

```
  12        12        13        10        11        12
 - 6       - 8       - 9       - 7       - 5       - 7
-----      -----     -----     -----     -----     -----
```

```
  14        14        11        12
 - 7       - 6       - 4       - 9
-----      -----     -----     -----
```

Anything's possible with practice!

Subtraction

Name _____

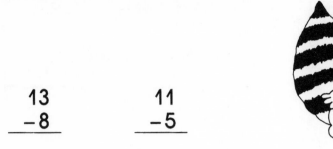

Total Problems	30
Problems Correct	_____

```
  13        11
 - 8       - 5
 ----      ----
```

```
  12        13        14         9        12        11
 - 4       - 5       - 9       - 6       - 8       - 2
 ----      ----      ----      ----      ----      ----
```

```
  11        12        13        10        12        13
 - 7       - 7       - 9       - 5       - 5       - 6
 ----      ----      ----      ----      ----      ----
```

```
  14        10        11        12        14         8
 - 7       - 3       - 3       - 9       - 8       - 4
 ----      ----      ----      ----      ----      ----
```

```
  13         6        10        12        11        14
 - 7       - 3       - 4       - 3       - 6       - 5
 ----      ----      ----      ----      ----      ----
```

```
  14        11        12        13
 - 6       - 4       - 6       - 4
 ----      ----      ----      ----
```

Practice = Success!

Subtraction

Name _____

Total Problems	30
Problems Correct	_____

```
 12        10
- 9       - 1
____      ____
```

```
 14        11        13         8        12        13
- 9       - 2       - 9       - 5       - 4       - 6
____      ____      ____      ____      ____      ____
```

```
  7        11        14        10        12        11
- 4       - 9       - 8       - 8       - 3       - 3
____      ____      ____      ____      ____      ____
```

```
 13        13        12        13        11         5
- 8       - 4       - 8       - 7       - 8       - 3
____      ____      ____      ____      ____      ____
```

```
 12        14        11         9        13        12
- 5       - 7       - 7       - 7       - 5       - 7
____      ____      ____      ____      ____      ____
```

```
 11        14         6        12
- 6       - 6       - 2       - 6
____      ____      ____      ____
```

Practice puts you on top!

Subtraction

Name _____

Total Problems	25
Problems Correct	_____

```
  13          15
 - 5         - 9
 ----        ----
```

```
  10          14          13          10          15
 - 4         - 6         - 6         - 9         - 7
 ----        ----        ----        ----        ----
```

```
  12          15          13          12          10
 - 5         - 5         - 7         - 7         - 6
 ----        ----        ----        ----        ----
```

```
  11          12          15          13          14
 - 6         - 4         - 6         - 9         - 5
 ----        ----        ----        ----        ----
```

```
  12          13          14          12          15
 - 9         - 8         - 7         - 6         - 9
 ----        ----        ----        ----        ----
```

```
  10          15          12
 - 5         - 8         - 8
 ----        ----        ----
```

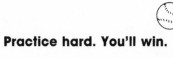

Practice hard. You'll win.

Subtraction

Name _____

Total Problems	30
Problems Correct	_____

```
  11        10
 - 6       - 6
 ____      ____
```

```
  16        14        13        15        14        16
 - 9       - 5       - 6       - 9       - 7       - 7
 ____      ____      ____      ____      ____      ____
```

```
  14        15        17        11        12        13
 - 6       - 7       - 9       - 8       - 9       - 9
 ____      ____      ____      ____      ____      ____
```

```
  17        12        12        10        14        15
 - 8       - 3       - 7       - 3       - 9       - 8
 ____      ____      ____      ____      ____      ____
```

```
  15        16        14        11        12        18
 - 6       - 9       - 5       - 9       - 6       - 9
 ____      ____      ____      ____      ____      ____
```

```
  13        16        10        14
 - 8       - 8       - 4       - 8
 ____      ____      ____      ____
```

With practice, you can do it!

Subtraction

Name _____

Total Problems	30
Problems Correct	_____

```
  17        12
 - 8       - 9
 ____      ____
```

```
  10        11        16        14        11        12
 - 8       - 2       - 8       - 9       - 8       - 6
 ____      ____      ____      ____      ____      ____
```

```
  13        15        11        14        17        12
 - 8       - 9       - 3       - 5       - 9       - 8
 ____      ____      ____      ____      ____      ____
```

```
  13        16        14        18        12        15
 - 4       - 7       - 8       - 9       - 5       - 6
 ____      ____      ____      ____      ____      ____
```

```
  14        10        15        13        11        13
 - 7       - 2       - 7       - 9       - 9       - 7
 ____      ____      ____      ____      ____      ____
```

Success ahoy! Just practice!

```
  10        16        15        14
 - 5       - 9       - 8       - 6
 ____      ____      ____      ____
```

Subtraction

Name _____

Total Problems	__30__
Problems Correct	_____

15 − 6 =

11 − 5 =

13 − 8 =   18 − 9 =   14 − 9 =

12 − 3 =   10 − 5 =   16 − 8 =

10 − 1 =   11 − 4 =   10 − 2 =

17 − 9 =   11 − 2 =   17 − 8 =

15 − 7 =   13 − 7 =   11 − 7 =

14 − 8 =   12 − 6 =   13 − 5 =

12 − 9 =   10 − 9 =   10 − 8 =

15 − 8 =   14 − 6 =   12 − 4 =

16 − 7 =   15 − 9 =   **Practice hard.**
                              You'll win.

12 − 5 =   11 − 8 =

Subtraction

Name _____

Total Problems	25
Problems Correct	_____

$$\begin{array}{r} 15 \\ -10 \\ \hline \end{array} \qquad \begin{array}{r} 83 \\ -52 \\ \hline \end{array}$$

$$\begin{array}{r} 69 \\ -45 \\ \hline \end{array} \quad \begin{array}{r} 64 \\ -41 \\ \hline \end{array} \quad \begin{array}{r} 42 \\ -11 \\ \hline \end{array} \quad \begin{array}{r} 39 \\ -16 \\ \hline \end{array} \quad \begin{array}{r} 53 \\ -30 \\ \hline \end{array}$$

$$\begin{array}{r} 78 \\ -45 \\ \hline \end{array} \quad \begin{array}{r} 85 \\ -52 \\ \hline \end{array} \quad \begin{array}{r} 90 \\ -40 \\ \hline \end{array} \quad \begin{array}{r} 88 \\ -11 \\ \hline \end{array} \quad \begin{array}{r} 73 \\ -35 \\ \hline \end{array}$$

$$\begin{array}{r} 86 \\ -53 \\ \hline \end{array} \quad \begin{array}{r} 57 \\ -46 \\ \hline \end{array} \quad \begin{array}{r} 53 \\ -33 \\ \hline \end{array} \quad \begin{array}{r} 64 \\ -41 \\ \hline \end{array} \quad \begin{array}{r} 63 \\ -60 \\ \hline \end{array}$$

$$\begin{array}{r} 75 \\ -31 \\ \hline \end{array} \quad \begin{array}{r} 69 \\ -36 \\ \hline \end{array} \quad \begin{array}{r} 77 \\ -52 \\ \hline \end{array} \quad \begin{array}{r} 86 \\ -35 \\ \hline \end{array} \quad \begin{array}{r} 58 \\ -28 \\ \hline \end{array}$$

$$\begin{array}{r} 50 \\ -10 \\ \hline \end{array} \quad \begin{array}{r} 86 \\ -55 \\ \hline \end{array} \quad \begin{array}{r} 49 \\ -26 \\ \hline \end{array}$$

Through practice you learn!

Subtraction

Name _____

Total Problems	25
Problems Correct	_____

```
  86        60
 -54       -30
```

```
  67        74        88        47        72
 -23       -45       -11       -17       -41
```

```
  66        85        38        69        99
 -23       -42       -28       -36       -40
```

```
  75        67        78        65        87
 -33       -62       -35       -41       -62
```

```
  50        83        96        37        80
 -10       -72       -23       -24       -30
```

```
  65        38        48
 -42       -16       -38
```

Practice and anything's possible!

© 1990 Instructional Fair, Inc.

Subtraction

Name _____

Total Problems	25
Problems Correct	_____

$$\begin{array}{r} 64 \\ -40 \\ \hline \end{array}$$
$$\begin{array}{r} 87 \\ -12 \\ \hline \end{array}$$

$$\begin{array}{r} 81 \\ -21 \\ \hline \end{array}$$
$$\begin{array}{r} 48 \\ -27 \\ \hline \end{array}$$
$$\begin{array}{r} 83 \\ -41 \\ \hline \end{array}$$
$$\begin{array}{r} 70 \\ -20 \\ \hline \end{array}$$
$$\begin{array}{r} 66 \\ -33 \\ \hline \end{array}$$

$$\begin{array}{r} 28 \\ -15 \\ \hline \end{array}$$
$$\begin{array}{r} 98 \\ -54 \\ \hline \end{array}$$
$$\begin{array}{r} 55 \\ -21 \\ \hline \end{array}$$
$$\begin{array}{r} 86 \\ -82 \\ \hline \end{array}$$
$$\begin{array}{r} 74 \\ -52 \\ \hline \end{array}$$

$$\begin{array}{r} 78 \\ -62 \\ \hline \end{array}$$
$$\begin{array}{r} 35 \\ -25 \\ \hline \end{array}$$
$$\begin{array}{r} 69 \\ -23 \\ \hline \end{array}$$
$$\begin{array}{r} 94 \\ -43 \\ \hline \end{array}$$
$$\begin{array}{r} 49 \\ -20 \\ \hline \end{array}$$

$$\begin{array}{r} 59 \\ -16 \\ \hline \end{array}$$
$$\begin{array}{r} 86 \\ -34 \\ \hline \end{array}$$
$$\begin{array}{r} 39 \\ -12 \\ \hline \end{array}$$
$$\begin{array}{r} 88 \\ -10 \\ \hline \end{array}$$
$$\begin{array}{r} 72 \\ -41 \\ \hline \end{array}$$

$$\begin{array}{r} 67 \\ -32 \\ \hline \end{array}$$
$$\begin{array}{r} 97 \\ -15 \\ \hline \end{array}$$
$$\begin{array}{r} 26 \\ -13 \\ \hline \end{array}$$

Practice! Practice! Practice!

Math IF8739

73

Subtraction

Name _____

Total Problems	25
Problems Correct	_____

```
  56          99
- 42        - 64
```

```
  78          33          74          66          39
- 34        - 12        - 72        - 30        - 26
```

```
  98          88          61          87          48
- 25        - 47        - 31        - 33        - 43
```

```
  66          97          83          28          59
- 11        - 27        - 21        - 10        - 22
```

```
  79          50          47          95          65
- 35        - 40        - 24        - 15        - 32
```

With practice, you can do it!

```
  29          96          92
- 25        - 13        - 61
```

Subtraction

Name _____

66	92
− 19	− 49

40	74	53	30	61
− 13	− 57	− 44	− 15	− 28

95	87	52	73	24
− 36	− 48	− 16	− 26	− 18

63	21	41	50	97
− 25	− 17	− 29	− 26	− 39

76	93	65	96	85
− 59	− 37	− 39	− 47	− 27

Practice makes perfect!

34	42	81
− 19	− 18	− 49

Subtraction

Name _____

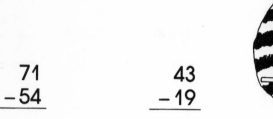

Total Problems	**25**
Problems Correct	_____

```
  71          43
- 54        - 19
____        ____
```

```
  46          81          57          90          26
- 29        - 36        - 39        - 18        - 18
____        ____        ____        ____        ____
```

```
  81          94          43          73          82
- 12        - 37        - 24        - 28        - 35
____        ____        ____        ____        ____
```

```
  57          91          74          62          33
- 28        - 26        - 19        - 13        - 27
____        ____        ____        ____        ____
```

```
  88          74          65          83          60
- 29        - 35        - 38        - 29        - 36
____        ____        ____        ____        ____
```

```
  91          52          80
- 45        - 24        - 49
____        ____        ____
```

Practice = Success!

Math IF8739

76

© 1990 Instructional Fair, Inc.

Subtraction

Name _____

Total Problems	25
Problems Correct	_____

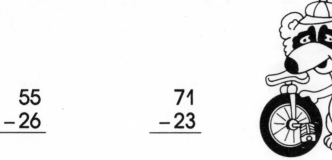

```
 55      71
-26     -23
```

```
 92      43      90      66      25
-37     -28     -36     -47     -19
```

```
 93      98      38      41      77
-25     -49     -19     -27     -49
```

```
 62      44      76      90      72
-23     -18     -29     -11     -16
```

```
 47      85      80      51      64
-38     -47     -37     -38     -26
```

Anything's possible with practice!

```
 83      92      97
-77     -28     -68
```

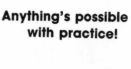

Subtraction

Name _____

Total Problems ___25___

Problems Correct _____

$$
\begin{array}{r} 61 \\ -47 \\ \hline \end{array}
\qquad
\begin{array}{r} 78 \\ -33 \\ \hline \end{array}
$$

$$
\begin{array}{r} 64 \\ -40 \\ \hline \end{array}
\quad
\begin{array}{r} 28 \\ -19 \\ \hline \end{array}
\quad
\begin{array}{r} 45 \\ -12 \\ \hline \end{array}
\quad
\begin{array}{r} 77 \\ -29 \\ \hline \end{array}
\quad
\begin{array}{r} 49 \\ -38 \\ \hline \end{array}
$$

$$
\begin{array}{r} 89 \\ -83 \\ \hline \end{array}
\quad
\begin{array}{r} 62 \\ -58 \\ \hline \end{array}
\quad
\begin{array}{r} 75 \\ -25 \\ \hline \end{array}
\quad
\begin{array}{r} 91 \\ -33 \\ \hline \end{array}
\quad
\begin{array}{r} 30 \\ -19 \\ \hline \end{array}
$$

$$
\begin{array}{r} 56 \\ -28 \\ \hline \end{array}
\quad
\begin{array}{r} 92 \\ -35 \\ \hline \end{array}
\quad
\begin{array}{r} 80 \\ -11 \\ \hline \end{array}
\quad
\begin{array}{r} 27 \\ -17 \\ \hline \end{array}
\quad
\begin{array}{r} 98 \\ -49 \\ \hline \end{array}
$$

$$
\begin{array}{r} 93 \\ -86 \\ \hline \end{array}
\quad
\begin{array}{r} 51 \\ -20 \\ \hline \end{array}
\quad
\begin{array}{r} 98 \\ -42 \\ \hline \end{array}
\quad
\begin{array}{r} 94 \\ -65 \\ \hline \end{array}
\quad
\begin{array}{r} 86 \\ -22 \\ \hline \end{array}
$$

$$
\begin{array}{r} 70 \\ -10 \\ \hline \end{array}
\quad
\begin{array}{r} 85 \\ -16 \\ \hline \end{array}
\quad
\begin{array}{r} 64 \\ -47 \\ \hline \end{array}
$$

With practice, you can do it!

Subtraction

Name _____

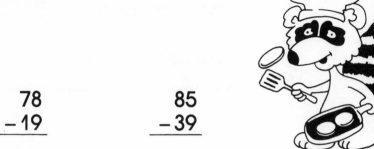

Total Problems	25
Problems Correct	_____

$$78 - 19$$ $$85 - 39$$

$$46 - 36$$ $$65 - 28$$ $$92 - 49$$ $$27 - 19$$ $$74 - 22$$

$$51 - 27$$ $$63 - 36$$ $$80 - 15$$ $$97 - 64$$ $$56 - 48$$

$$44 - 29$$ $$79 - 58$$ $$87 - 48$$ $$34 - 26$$ $$94 - 15$$

$$90 - 34$$ $$53 - 45$$ $$32 - 18$$ $$89 - 12$$ $$81 - 35$$

Practice brings success!

$$78 - 43$$ $$42 - 13$$ $$50 - 30$$

    © 1990 Instructional Fair, Inc.

Subtraction

Name _____

Total Problems	__25__
Problems Correct	_____

```
  129        976
 - 26       -432
```

```
  697        458        856        379        702
 -272       -141       -114       -163       -102
```

```
  216         94        885        196         98
 - 13        -72       -330       - 81        -46
```

```
  678        327        180        997        364
 -162        -23       -140       -354       - 60
```

```
  111         62        143        925        300
 - 10        -31        -23        -24       -100
```

```
  833        278        899
 -121        -60       -275
```

Practice hard. You'll win.

Subtraction

Name _____

Total Problems	**25**
Problems Correct	_____

```
  454        675
- 120      - 125
```

```
  158        500        996        770        195
- 147      - 400      - 413      - 350      - 181
```

```
  659        332        898        297        879
- 357      - 111      - 423      - 152      - 110
```

```
  780        819        529        776        490
- 130      - 209      - 216      - 725      - 360
```

```
  245        657        388        427        948
- 132      - 122      - 266      - 212      - 532
```

```
  730        897        968
- 130      - 535      - 721
```

Practice makes perfect!

Addition and Subtraction

Name _____

Total Problems	25
Problems Correct	_____

$$\begin{array}{r} 5 \\ +0 \\ \hline \end{array} \qquad \begin{array}{r} 2 \\ +2 \\ \hline \end{array}$$

$$\begin{array}{r} 2 \\ +3 \\ \hline \end{array} \qquad \begin{array}{r} 4 \\ +1 \\ \hline \end{array} \qquad \begin{array}{r} 3 \\ +3 \\ \hline \end{array} \qquad \begin{array}{r} 6 \\ +0 \\ \hline \end{array} \qquad \begin{array}{r} 5 \\ +1 \\ \hline \end{array}$$

$$\begin{array}{r} 3 \\ +1 \\ \hline \end{array} \qquad \begin{array}{r} 2 \\ +0 \\ \hline \end{array} \qquad \begin{array}{r} 0 \\ +0 \\ \hline \end{array} \qquad \begin{array}{r} 1 \\ +4 \\ \hline \end{array} \qquad \begin{array}{r} 1 \\ +1 \\ \hline \end{array}$$

$$\begin{array}{r} 6 \\ -6 \\ \hline \end{array} \qquad \begin{array}{r} 4 \\ -2 \\ \hline \end{array} \qquad \begin{array}{r} 2 \\ -1 \\ \hline \end{array} \qquad \begin{array}{r} 3 \\ -0 \\ \hline \end{array} \qquad \begin{array}{r} 5 \\ -3 \\ \hline \end{array}$$

$$\begin{array}{r} 0 \\ -0 \\ \hline \end{array} \qquad \begin{array}{r} 6 \\ -3 \\ \hline \end{array} \qquad \begin{array}{r} 5 \\ -2 \\ \hline \end{array} \qquad \begin{array}{r} 2 \\ -2 \\ \hline \end{array} \qquad \begin{array}{r} 5 \\ -4 \\ \hline \end{array}$$

Practice puts you on top!

$$\begin{array}{r} 6 \\ -2 \\ \hline \end{array} \qquad \begin{array}{r} 4 \\ -3 \\ \hline \end{array} \qquad \begin{array}{r} 6 \\ -5 \\ \hline \end{array}$$

Math IF8739

82

Addition and Subtraction

Name _____

Total Problems	25
Problems Correct	_____

```
  6        1
 -3       +3
___      ___
```

```
  3        0        3        6        2
 -0       +6       +1       -2       -1
___      ___      ___      ___      ___
```

```
  3        0        6        2        5
 +3       +0       -5       +3       +4
___      ___      ___      ___      ___
```

```
  2        2        5        4        2
 -1       +2       -4       +2       +3
___      ___      ___      ___      ___
```

```
  6        0        1        2        4
 -4       +5       +4       +2       -3
___      ___      ___      ___      ___
```

Practice = Success!

```
  6        1        2
 -0       +5       +4
___      ___      ___
```

Addition and Subtraction

Name _____

Total Problems	30
Problems Correct	_____

$2 - 1 =$

$5 - 4 =$

$1 + 3 =$ $5 - 3 =$ $5 - 1 =$

$6 - 3 =$ $2 + 2 =$ $2 + 4 =$

$3 - 0 =$ $4 + 2 =$ $5 + 0 =$

$0 + 6 =$ $6 - 4 =$ $5 - 2 =$

$3 + 1 =$ $0 + 5 =$ $1 + 2 =$

$6 - 2 =$ $1 + 4 =$ $6 + 0 =$

$2 - 1 =$ $2 + 3 =$ $0 - 0 =$

$3 + 3 =$ $4 - 3 =$ $4 - 1 =$

Practice makes perfect!

$0 - 0 =$ $6 - 0 =$

$6 - 5 =$ $1 + 5 =$

Addition and Subtraction

Name _____

Total Problems	25
Problems Correct	_____

$$\begin{array}{r} 3 \\ +5 \\ \hline \end{array} \qquad \begin{array}{r} 9 \\ +1 \\ \hline \end{array}$$

$$\begin{array}{r} 6 \\ +3 \\ \hline \end{array} \quad \begin{array}{r} 8 \\ +2 \\ \hline \end{array} \quad \begin{array}{r} 7 \\ +3 \\ \hline \end{array} \quad \begin{array}{r} 6 \\ +2 \\ \hline \end{array} \quad \begin{array}{r} 7 \\ +1 \\ \hline \end{array}$$

$$\begin{array}{r} 6 \\ +4 \\ \hline \end{array} \quad \begin{array}{r} 9 \\ +0 \\ \hline \end{array} \quad \begin{array}{r} 4 \\ +4 \\ \hline \end{array} \quad \begin{array}{r} 8 \\ +1 \\ \hline \end{array} \quad \begin{array}{r} 5 \\ +4 \\ \hline \end{array}$$

$$\begin{array}{r} 9 \\ -5 \\ \hline \end{array} \quad \begin{array}{r} 6 \\ -2 \\ \hline \end{array} \quad \begin{array}{r} 8 \\ -5 \\ \hline \end{array} \quad \begin{array}{r} 10 \\ -2 \\ \hline \end{array} \quad \begin{array}{r} 7 \\ -7 \\ \hline \end{array}$$

$$\begin{array}{r} 6 \\ -3 \\ \hline \end{array} \quad \begin{array}{r} 5 \\ -1 \\ \hline \end{array} \quad \begin{array}{r} 9 \\ -0 \\ \hline \end{array} \quad \begin{array}{r} 10 \\ -5 \\ \hline \end{array} \quad \begin{array}{r} 9 \\ -6 \\ \hline \end{array}$$

$$\begin{array}{r} 8 \\ -4 \\ \hline \end{array} \qquad \begin{array}{r} 10 \\ -6 \\ \hline \end{array} \qquad \begin{array}{r} 9 \\ -4 \\ \hline \end{array}$$

Practice and anything's possible!

Addition and Subtraction

Name _____

Total Problems	25
Problems Correct	_____

$$
\begin{array}{r} 6 \\ +4 \\ \hline \end{array}
\qquad
\begin{array}{r} 9 \\ -3 \\ \hline \end{array}
$$

$$
\begin{array}{r} 5 \\ +5 \\ \hline \end{array}
\qquad
\begin{array}{r} 8 \\ -2 \\ \hline \end{array}
\qquad
\begin{array}{r} 10 \\ -4 \\ \hline \end{array}
\qquad
\begin{array}{r} 2 \\ +7 \\ \hline \end{array}
\qquad
\begin{array}{r} 8 \\ -5 \\ \hline \end{array}
$$

$$
\begin{array}{r} 9 \\ -6 \\ \hline \end{array}
\qquad
\begin{array}{r} 5 \\ +3 \\ \hline \end{array}
\qquad
\begin{array}{r} 9 \\ -4 \\ \hline \end{array}
\qquad
\begin{array}{r} 8 \\ +2 \\ \hline \end{array}
\qquad
\begin{array}{r} 7 \\ -4 \\ \hline \end{array}
$$

$$
\begin{array}{r} 6 \\ +3 \\ \hline \end{array}
\qquad
\begin{array}{r} 10 \\ -10 \\ \hline \end{array}
\qquad
\begin{array}{r} 5 \\ +1 \\ \hline \end{array}
\qquad
\begin{array}{r} 5 \\ +4 \\ \hline \end{array}
\qquad
\begin{array}{r} 5 \\ -4 \\ \hline \end{array}
$$

$$
\begin{array}{r} 10 \\ -4 \\ \hline \end{array}
\qquad
\begin{array}{r} 7 \\ +3 \\ \hline \end{array}
\qquad
\begin{array}{r} 2 \\ +6 \\ \hline \end{array}
\qquad
\begin{array}{r} 8 \\ -7 \\ \hline \end{array}
\qquad
\begin{array}{r} 6 \\ -3 \\ \hline \end{array}
$$

Through practice you learn!

$$
\begin{array}{r} 9 \\ +1 \\ \hline \end{array}
\qquad
\begin{array}{r} 8 \\ -4 \\ \hline \end{array}
\qquad
\begin{array}{r} 3 \\ +4 \\ \hline \end{array}
$$

Addition and Subtraction

Name _____

Total Problems	30
Problems Correct	_____

$8 - 4 =$

$6 + 3 =$

$10 - 10 =$ $3 + 4 =$ $5 + 4 =$

$5 + 1 =$ $5 + 5 =$ $6 - 4 =$

$4 + 5 =$ $8 - 2 =$ $7 + 3 =$

$5 - 4 =$ $10 - 6 =$ $9 - 2 =$

$10 - 4 =$ $2 + 7 =$ $8 - 6 =$

$7 + 3 =$ $8 - 5 =$ $5 + 3 =$

$2 + 6 =$ $6 + 4 =$ $10 - 0 =$

$8 - 7 =$ $9 - 3 =$ $9 - 1 =$

Practice hard. You'll win.

$6 - 3 =$ $10 - 10 =$

$9 + 1 =$ $5 + 1 =$

Math IF8739   87   © 1990 Instructional Fair. Inc.

Addition and Subtraction

Name _____

Total Problems	35
Problems Correct	_____

```
   6        8        5
 +3       -1       -2
____     ____     ____
```

```
   4       10        1        6        5        0        2
 +3       -7       +5       -3       -1       +7       +1
____     ____     ____     ____     ____     ____     ____
```

```
   9        4        5        7        8        2        5
 -6       -2       +5       -5       -6       +7       -2
____     ____     ____     ____     ____     ____     ____
```

```
   7        2        9        5        6        3        2
 -4       +3       -8       +2       -2       -1       +8
____     ____     ____     ____     ____     ____     ____
```

```
   4        6        8        5        9        4       10
 +2       -4       -4       +3       -5       +4       -5
____     ____     ____     ____     ____     ____     ____
```

Practice!
Practice!
Practice!

```
   4        8        7        1
 +1       -0       -7       +9
____     ____     ____     ____
```

Addition and Subtraction

Name _____

Total Problems	25
Problems Correct	_____

$$
\begin{array}{r} 10 \\ -5 \\ \hline \end{array}
\qquad
\begin{array}{r} 9 \\ +2 \\ \hline \end{array}
$$

$$
\begin{array}{r} 9 \\ -2 \\ \hline \end{array}
\quad
\begin{array}{r} 4 \\ +7 \\ \hline \end{array}
\quad
\begin{array}{r} 5 \\ +6 \\ \hline \end{array}
\quad
\begin{array}{r} 11 \\ -9 \\ \hline \end{array}
\quad
\begin{array}{r} 10 \\ -6 \\ \hline \end{array}
$$

$$
\begin{array}{r} 7 \\ +1 \\ \hline \end{array}
\quad
\begin{array}{r} 8 \\ +3 \\ \hline \end{array}
\quad
\begin{array}{r} 11 \\ -7 \\ \hline \end{array}
\quad
\begin{array}{r} 10 \\ -4 \\ \hline \end{array}
\quad
\begin{array}{r} 5 \\ +5 \\ \hline \end{array}
$$

$$
\begin{array}{r} 8 \\ +2 \\ \hline \end{array}
\quad
\begin{array}{r} 10 \\ +1 \\ \hline \end{array}
\quad
\begin{array}{r} 11 \\ -4 \\ \hline \end{array}
\quad
\begin{array}{r} 7 \\ +3 \\ \hline \end{array}
\quad
\begin{array}{r} 10 \\ -3 \\ \hline \end{array}
$$

$$
\begin{array}{r} 10 \\ -7 \\ \hline \end{array}
\quad
\begin{array}{r} 11 \\ -6 \\ \hline \end{array}
\quad
\begin{array}{r} 6 \\ +4 \\ \hline \end{array}
\quad
\begin{array}{r} 10 \\ -8 \\ \hline \end{array}
\quad
\begin{array}{r} 7 \\ +3 \\ \hline \end{array}
$$

$$
\begin{array}{r} 9 \\ +1 \\ \hline \end{array}
\quad
\begin{array}{r} 11 \\ -2 \\ \hline \end{array}
\quad
\begin{array}{r} 5 \\ +4 \\ \hline \end{array}
$$

Practice makes perfect!

Addition and Subtraction

Name _____

Total Problems	__25__
Problems Correct	_____

```
  7        12
+ 4       - 6
___       ___
```

```
  3         6        12         5        11
+ 8       + 6       - 4       + 5       - 3
___       ___       ___       ___       ___
```

```
 11         9         7        12         8
- 6       + 2       + 5       - 3       + 2
___       ___       ___       ___       ___
```

```
 10         6        12         7        11
- 4       + 5       - 2       + 3       - 5
___       ___       ___       ___       ___
```

```
 11         8        10         9        11
- 7       + 4       - 7       + 3       - 8
___       ___       ___       ___       ___
```

Practice brings success!

```
  5        12        11
+ 5       - 5       - 4
___       ___       ___
```

Addition and Subtraction

Name _____

Total Problems	30
Problems Correct	_____

$$\begin{array}{r} 1 \\ +9 \\ \hline \end{array} \qquad \begin{array}{r} 10 \\ -6 \\ \hline \end{array}$$

$$\begin{array}{r} 14 \\ -9 \\ \hline \end{array} \quad \begin{array}{r} 3 \\ +8 \\ \hline \end{array} \quad \begin{array}{r} 14 \\ -7 \\ \hline \end{array} \quad \begin{array}{r} 6 \\ +4 \\ \hline \end{array} \quad \begin{array}{r} 13 \\ -7 \\ \hline \end{array} \quad \begin{array}{r} 2 \\ +9 \\ \hline \end{array}$$

$$\begin{array}{r} 13 \\ -8 \\ \hline \end{array} \quad \begin{array}{r} 3 \\ +9 \\ \hline \end{array} \quad \begin{array}{r} 11 \\ -8 \\ \hline \end{array} \quad \begin{array}{r} 8 \\ +5 \\ \hline \end{array} \quad \begin{array}{r} 10 \\ -1 \\ \hline \end{array} \quad \begin{array}{r} 12 \\ -6 \\ \hline \end{array}$$

$$\begin{array}{r} 6 \\ +7 \\ \hline \end{array} \quad \begin{array}{r} 11 \\ -6 \\ \hline \end{array} \quad \begin{array}{r} 4 \\ +8 \\ \hline \end{array} \quad \begin{array}{r} 10 \\ -2 \\ \hline \end{array} \quad \begin{array}{r} 5 \\ +6 \\ \hline \end{array} \quad \begin{array}{r} 12 \\ -3 \\ \hline \end{array}$$

$$\begin{array}{r} 7 \\ +7 \\ \hline \end{array} \quad \begin{array}{r} 12 \\ -5 \\ \hline \end{array} \quad \begin{array}{r} 6 \\ +8 \\ \hline \end{array} \quad \begin{array}{r} 5 \\ +9 \\ \hline \end{array} \quad \begin{array}{r} 13 \\ -4 \\ \hline \end{array} \quad \begin{array}{r} 5 \\ +7 \\ \hline \end{array}$$

**Practice hard.
You'll win!**

$$\begin{array}{r} 9 \\ +2 \\ \hline \end{array} \quad \begin{array}{r} 9 \\ +4 \\ \hline \end{array} \quad \begin{array}{r} 14 \\ -8 \\ \hline \end{array} \quad \begin{array}{r} 12 \\ -7 \\ \hline \end{array}$$

Addition and Subtraction

Name _____

Total Problems	__30__
Problems Correct	_____

```
  15        9
 -9       +9
_____    _____
```

```
   8       17       15       11        6       16
  +9       -9       -8       -2       +9       -7
_____    _____    _____    _____    _____    _____
```

```
  12        6       16        7       14        9
  -9       +7       -8       +8       -6       +2
_____    _____    _____    _____    _____    _____
```

```
  15        8       18        9        7       13
  -6       +8       -9       +3       +9       -5
_____    _____    _____    _____    _____    _____
```

```
   6        8       13        9        9       15
  +5       +6       -6       +7       +8       -7
_____    _____    _____    _____    _____    _____
```

Practice brings success!

```
   9       17        8       16
  +6       -8       +7       -9
_____    _____    _____    _____
```

Addition and Subtraction

Name _____

Total Problems	28
Problems Correct	_____

$6 + 8 =$

$8 + 6 =$

$14 - 6 =$ $8 + 9 =$ $7 + 9 =$

$14 - 8 =$ $9 + 8 =$ $9 + 7 =$

                 $17 - 9 =$ $16 - 9 =$

$6 + 9 =$ $17 - 8 =$ $16 - 7 =$

$9 + 6 =$

$15 - 9 =$

$15 - 6 =$ $5 + 8 =$ $7 + 5 =$

                 $8 + 5 =$ $5 + 7 =$

$3 + 8 =$ $13 - 8 =$ $12 - 5 =$

$8 + 3 =$ $13 - 5 =$ $12 - 7 =$

$11 - 8 =$

$11 - 3 =$

Practice hard. You'll win.

Addition and Subtraction

Name _____

Total Problems	25
Problems Correct	_____

```
  30        96
+ 18      - 30
```

```
  72        58        36        84        78
+ 13      - 16      + 33      - 20      - 63
```

```
  87        51        77        40        96
- 44      + 37      - 35      + 30      - 50
```

```
  58        56        60        89        23
+ 31      - 56      + 30      - 62      + 34
```

```
  77        45        86        24        49
- 40      + 21      - 45      + 43      - 26
```

```
  97        30        73
- 22      + 47      - 40
```

Practice = Success!

Math IF8739

94

© 1990 Instructional Fair, Inc.

Addition and Subtraction

Name _____

Total Problems	25
Problems Correct	_____

$$\begin{array}{r} 54 \\ +34 \\ \hline \end{array}$$
$$\begin{array}{r} 16 \\ -11 \\ \hline \end{array}$$

$$\begin{array}{r} 62 \\ -41 \\ \hline \end{array}$$
$$\begin{array}{r} 62 \\ +20 \\ \hline \end{array}$$
$$\begin{array}{r} 47 \\ +32 \\ \hline \end{array}$$
$$\begin{array}{r} 65 \\ -45 \\ \hline \end{array}$$
$$\begin{array}{r} 48 \\ -15 \\ \hline \end{array}$$

$$\begin{array}{r} 36 \\ +40 \\ \hline \end{array}$$
$$\begin{array}{r} 17 \\ +41 \\ \hline \end{array}$$
$$\begin{array}{r} 69 \\ -28 \\ \hline \end{array}$$
$$\begin{array}{r} 64 \\ +32 \\ \hline \end{array}$$
$$\begin{array}{r} 76 \\ -52 \\ \hline \end{array}$$

$$\begin{array}{r} 86 \\ -62 \\ \hline \end{array}$$
$$\begin{array}{r} 50 \\ -30 \\ \hline \end{array}$$
$$\begin{array}{r} 32 \\ +32 \\ \hline \end{array}$$
$$\begin{array}{r} 83 \\ -72 \\ \hline \end{array}$$
$$\begin{array}{r} 60 \\ +20 \\ \hline \end{array}$$

$$\begin{array}{r} 88 \\ -11 \\ \hline \end{array}$$
$$\begin{array}{r} 61 \\ +38 \\ \hline \end{array}$$
$$\begin{array}{r} 35 \\ +43 \\ \hline \end{array}$$
$$\begin{array}{r} 87 \\ -52 \\ \hline \end{array}$$

Practice! Practice! Practice!

$$\begin{array}{r} 30 \\ +29 \\ \hline \end{array}$$
$$\begin{array}{r} 45 \\ -42 \\ \hline \end{array}$$
$$\begin{array}{r} 62 \\ +35 \\ \hline \end{array}$$
$$\begin{array}{r} 40 \\ +29 \\ \hline \end{array}$$

Math IF8739

Addition and Subtraction

Name _____

Total Problems ___25___

Problems Correct _____

$$\begin{array}{r} 75 \\ -25 \\ \hline \end{array} \qquad \begin{array}{r} 36 \\ +25 \\ \hline \end{array}$$

$$\begin{array}{r} 27 \\ -17 \\ \hline \end{array} \quad \begin{array}{r} 15 \\ +19 \\ \hline \end{array} \quad \begin{array}{r} 50 \\ -22 \\ \hline \end{array} \quad \begin{array}{r} 75 \\ -37 \\ \hline \end{array} \quad \begin{array}{r} 23 \\ +75 \\ \hline \end{array}$$

$$\begin{array}{r} 79 \\ +10 \\ \hline \end{array} \quad \begin{array}{r} 97 \\ -84 \\ \hline \end{array} \quad \begin{array}{r} 51 \\ +28 \\ \hline \end{array} \quad \begin{array}{r} 43 \\ -24 \\ \hline \end{array} \quad \begin{array}{r} 61 \\ +19 \\ \hline \end{array}$$

$$\begin{array}{r} 96 \\ -18 \\ \hline \end{array} \quad \begin{array}{r} 82 \\ -46 \\ \hline \end{array} \quad \begin{array}{r} 33 \\ +49 \\ \hline \end{array} \quad \begin{array}{r} 66 \\ +22 \\ \hline \end{array} \quad \begin{array}{r} 86 \\ -24 \\ \hline \end{array}$$

$$\begin{array}{r} 62 \\ -19 \\ \hline \end{array} \quad \begin{array}{r} 29 \\ +29 \\ \hline \end{array} \quad \begin{array}{r} 39 \\ -16 \\ \hline \end{array} \quad \begin{array}{r} 53 \\ -24 \\ \hline \end{array} \quad \begin{array}{r} 80 \\ +12 \\ \hline \end{array}$$

Through practice you learn!

$$\begin{array}{r} 40 \\ +30 \\ \hline \end{array} \quad \begin{array}{r} 71 \\ -30 \\ \hline \end{array} \quad \begin{array}{r} 79 \\ +18 \\ \hline \end{array}$$

Math IF8739

Addition and Subtraction

Name _____

Total Problems	25
Problems Correct	_____

```
   66        16
 - 40      + 19
```

```
   27        88        21        91        52
 + 16      - 63      + 71      - 25      + 37
```

```
   83        32        59        48        70
 + 14      - 17      - 45      + 47      - 11
```

```
   33        41        42        97        68
 - 15      + 50      + 37      - 34      - 49
```

```
   76        47        59        54        24
 + 22      + 13      + 26      - 27      - 14
```

```
   74        79        62
 - 50      + 18      + 23
```

Practice hard.

You'll win!

Addition and Subtraction

Name _____

Total Problems	25
Problems Correct	_____

```
   127        932
 + 611      - 410
 ------     ------
```

```
   319        455        840        254        821
 - 219      + 102      - 340      + 515      - 710
 ------     ------     ------     ------     ------
```

```
   488        671        285        178        867
 + 400      - 361      + 214      - 156      + 131
 ------     ------     ------     ------     ------
```

```
   376        747        163        500        612
 + 501      - 632      + 205      - 300      + 174
 ------     ------     ------     ------     ------
```

```
   599        253        584        326        427
 - 127      + 403      - 241      + 211      - 227
 ------     ------     ------     ------     ------
```

```
   550        157        737
 - 110      + 132      - 331
 ------     ------     ------
```

Anything's possible with practice!

Multiplication

Name _____

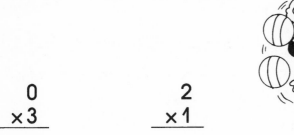

Total Problems	25
Problems Correct	_____

```
  0        2
 ×3       ×1
```

```
  2        3        3        0        1
 ×2       ×5       ×1       ×3       ×2
```

```
  2        3        1        2        0
 ×5       ×4       ×1       ×3       ×0
```

```
  0        2        1        3        1
 ×1       ×4       ×5       ×2       ×0
```

```
  3        1        4        2        0
 ×3       ×3       ×3       ×5       ×2
```

Practice! Practice! Practice!

```
  1        4        5
 ×4       ×2       ×2
```

Multiplication

Name _____

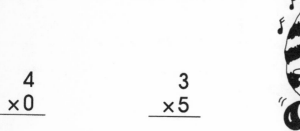

Total Problems	25
Problems Correct	_____

$$\begin{array}{r} 4 \\ \times 0 \\ \hline \end{array} \qquad \begin{array}{r} 3 \\ \times 5 \\ \hline \end{array}$$

$$\begin{array}{r} 3 \\ \times 3 \\ \hline \end{array} \quad \begin{array}{r} 5 \\ \times 1 \\ \hline \end{array} \quad \begin{array}{r} 4 \\ \times 3 \\ \hline \end{array} \quad \begin{array}{r} 3 \\ \times 1 \\ \hline \end{array} \quad \begin{array}{r} 4 \\ \times 5 \\ \hline \end{array}$$

$$\begin{array}{r} 3 \\ \times 0 \\ \hline \end{array} \quad \begin{array}{r} 4 \\ \times 2 \\ \hline \end{array} \quad \begin{array}{r} 5 \\ \times 4 \\ \hline \end{array} \quad \begin{array}{r} 3 \\ \times 2 \\ \hline \end{array} \quad \begin{array}{r} 5 \\ \times 3 \\ \hline \end{array}$$

$$\begin{array}{r} 3 \\ \times 3 \\ \hline \end{array} \quad \begin{array}{r} 4 \\ \times 3 \\ \hline \end{array} \quad \begin{array}{r} 3 \\ \times 2 \\ \hline \end{array} \quad \begin{array}{r} 5 \\ \times 0 \\ \hline \end{array} \quad \begin{array}{r} 4 \\ \times 1 \\ \hline \end{array}$$

$$\begin{array}{r} 5 \\ \times 2 \\ \hline \end{array} \quad \begin{array}{r} 4 \\ \times 3 \\ \hline \end{array} \quad \begin{array}{r} 5 \\ \times 1 \\ \hline \end{array} \quad \begin{array}{r} 3 \\ \times 4 \\ \hline \end{array} \quad \begin{array}{r} 4 \\ \times 0 \\ \hline \end{array}$$

Practice and anything's possible!

$$\begin{array}{r} 3 \\ \times 0 \\ \hline \end{array} \quad \begin{array}{r} 5 \\ \times 5 \\ \hline \end{array} \quad \begin{array}{r} 4 \\ \times 4 \\ \hline \end{array}$$

Math IF8739

Multiplication

Name _____

Total Problems	30
Problems Correct	_____

```
  4        2
 ×3       ×1
```

```
  2        1        5        4        2        3
 ×4       ×0       ×3       ×5       ×0       ×3
```

```
  3        5        4        1        3        1
 ×1       ×4       ×2       ×1       ×5       ×4
```

```
  4        2        1        3        2        5
 ×1       ×5       ×5       ×4       ×3       ×5
```

```
  5        3        0        5        1        4
 ×2       ×2       ×1       ×0       ×2       ×5
```

Practice = Success!

```
  3        2        1        5
 ×0       ×2       ×3       ×1
```

Multiplication

Name _____

Total Problems	30
Problems Correct	_____

$2 \times 1 =$

$4 \times 1 =$

$1 \times 1 =$ $0 \times 0 =$ $2 \times 5 =$

$0 \times 1 =$ $3 \times 3 =$ $4 \times 5 =$

$3 \times 5 =$ $4 \times 4 =$ $0 \times 4 =$

$4 \times 2 =$ $1 \times 2 =$ $2 \times 2 =$

$2 \times 4 =$ $0 \times 5 =$ $5 \times 2 =$

$3 \times 2 =$ $2 \times 3 =$ $1 \times 3 =$

$4 \times 3 =$ $5 \times 3 =$ $0 \times 2 =$

$0 \times 3 =$ $5 \times 5 =$ $3 \times 1 =$

$5 \times 4 =$ $1 \times 4 =$ **With practice, you can do it!**

$1 \times 5 =$ $3 \times 4 =$

Answer Key

Page 1

Addition

Name _____

Total Problems	23
Problems Correct	___

$\begin{array}{r}1\\+3\\\hline 4\end{array}$ $\begin{array}{r}2\\+4\\\hline 6\end{array}$

$\begin{array}{r}0\\+5\\\hline 5\end{array}$ $\begin{array}{r}3\\+2\\\hline 5\end{array}$ $\begin{array}{r}0\\+0\\\hline 0\end{array}$ $\begin{array}{r}5\\+1\\\hline 6\end{array}$ $\begin{array}{r}2\\+2\\\hline 4\end{array}$

$\begin{array}{r}1\\+1\\\hline 2\end{array}$ $\begin{array}{r}4\\+1\\\hline 5\end{array}$ $\begin{array}{r}3\\+3\\\hline 6\end{array}$ $\begin{array}{r}2\\+1\\\hline 3\end{array}$ $\begin{array}{r}0\\+6\\\hline 6\end{array}$

$\begin{array}{r}3\\+1\\\hline 4\end{array}$ $\begin{array}{r}5\\+0\\\hline 5\end{array}$ $\begin{array}{r}4\\+2\\\hline 6\end{array}$ $\begin{array}{r}3\\+0\\\hline 3\end{array}$ $\begin{array}{r}1\\+5\\\hline 6\end{array}$

$\begin{array}{r}4\\+0\\\hline 4\end{array}$ $\begin{array}{r}1\\+2\\\hline 3\end{array}$ $\begin{array}{r}6\\+0\\\hline 6\end{array}$

With practice, you can do it!

$\begin{array}{r}0\\+2\\\hline 2\end{array}$ $\begin{array}{r}2\\+3\\\hline 5\end{array}$ $\begin{array}{r}3\\+0\\\hline 3\end{array}$

Page 2

Addition

Name _____

Total Problems	30
Problems Correct	___

$2 + 1 = 3$

$4 + 0 = 4$

$1 + 2 = 3$ $0 + 6 = 6$ $0 + 5 = 5$

$6 + 0 = 6$ $3 + 2 = 5$ $2 + 4 = 6$

$1 + 4 = 5$ $0 + 0 = 0$ $1 + 3 = 4$

$0 + 3 = 3$ $2 + 3 = 5$ $0 + 2 = 2$

$3 + 1 = 4$ $5 + 1 = 6$ $2 + 1 = 3$

$5 + 0 = 5$ $2 + 0 = 2$ $4 + 1 = 5$

$4 + 2 = 6$ $6 + 0 = 6$ $0 + 4 = 4$

$2 + 3 = 5$ $2 + 2 = 4$ $5 + 1 = 6$

Practice = Success!

$1 + 1 = 2$ $1 + 5 = 6$

$3 + 3 = 6$ $3 + 0 = 3$

Page 3

Addition

Name _____

Total Problems	25
Problems Correct	___

$\begin{array}{r}4\\+2\\\hline 6\end{array}$ $\begin{array}{r}0\\+7\\\hline 7\end{array}$

$\begin{array}{r}2\\+3\\\hline 5\end{array}$ $\begin{array}{r}4\\+3\\\hline 7\end{array}$ $\begin{array}{r}5\\+1\\\hline 6\end{array}$ $\begin{array}{r}2\\+4\\\hline 6\end{array}$ $\begin{array}{r}5\\+2\\\hline 7\end{array}$

$\begin{array}{r}6\\+0\\\hline 6\end{array}$ $\begin{array}{r}2\\+2\\\hline 4\end{array}$ $\begin{array}{r}5\\+0\\\hline 5\end{array}$ $\begin{array}{r}3\\+3\\\hline 6\end{array}$ $\begin{array}{r}2\\+1\\\hline 3\end{array}$

$\begin{array}{r}2\\+0\\\hline 2\end{array}$ $\begin{array}{r}1\\+2\\\hline 3\end{array}$ $\begin{array}{r}3\\+1\\\hline 4\end{array}$ $\begin{array}{r}6\\+1\\\hline 7\end{array}$ $\begin{array}{r}4\\+1\\\hline 5\end{array}$

$\begin{array}{r}2\\+5\\\hline 7\end{array}$ $\begin{array}{r}0\\+5\\\hline 5\end{array}$ $\begin{array}{r}7\\+0\\\hline 7\end{array}$ $\begin{array}{r}1\\+5\\\hline 6\end{array}$ $\begin{array}{r}3\\+4\\\hline 7\end{array}$

Practice and anything's possible!

$\begin{array}{r}3\\+2\\\hline 5\end{array}$ $\begin{array}{r}0\\+0\\\hline 0\end{array}$ $\begin{array}{r}1\\+6\\\hline 7\end{array}$

Page 4

Addition

Name _____

Total Problems	35
Problems Correct	___

$\begin{array}{r}3\\+7\\\hline 10\end{array}$ $\begin{array}{r}2\\+3\\\hline 5\end{array}$ $\begin{array}{r}1\\+4\\\hline 5\end{array}$

$\begin{array}{r}2\\+4\\\hline 6\end{array}$ $\begin{array}{r}5\\+4\\\hline 9\end{array}$ $\begin{array}{r}6\\+2\\\hline 8\end{array}$ $\begin{array}{r}3\\+5\\\hline 8\end{array}$ $\begin{array}{r}10\\+0\\\hline 10\end{array}$ $\begin{array}{r}2\\+8\\\hline 10\end{array}$ $\begin{array}{r}3\\+3\\\hline 6\end{array}$

$\begin{array}{r}0\\+1\\\hline 1\end{array}$ $\begin{array}{r}6\\+4\\\hline 10\end{array}$ $\begin{array}{r}5\\+0\\\hline 5\end{array}$ $\begin{array}{r}5\\+3\\\hline 8\end{array}$ $\begin{array}{r}7\\+3\\\hline 10\end{array}$ $\begin{array}{r}1\\+8\\\hline 9\end{array}$ $\begin{array}{r}2\\+2\\\hline 4\end{array}$

$\begin{array}{r}7\\+2\\\hline 9\end{array}$ $\begin{array}{r}4\\+4\\\hline 8\end{array}$ $\begin{array}{r}1\\+2\\\hline 3\end{array}$ $\begin{array}{r}9\\+1\\\hline 10\end{array}$ $\begin{array}{r}3\\+6\\\hline 9\end{array}$ $\begin{array}{r}6\\+1\\\hline 7\end{array}$ $\begin{array}{r}5\\+2\\\hline 7\end{array}$

$\begin{array}{r}8\\+2\\\hline 10\end{array}$ $\begin{array}{r}4\\+3\\\hline 7\end{array}$ $\begin{array}{r}2\\+7\\\hline 9\end{array}$ $\begin{array}{r}0\\+3\\\hline 3\end{array}$ $\begin{array}{r}2\\+5\\\hline 7\end{array}$ $\begin{array}{r}0\\+9\\\hline 9\end{array}$ $\begin{array}{r}5\\+1\\\hline 6\end{array}$

Practice makes perfect!

$\begin{array}{r}6\\+3\\\hline 9\end{array}$ $\begin{array}{r}2\\+6\\\hline 8\end{array}$ $\begin{array}{r}5\\+5\\\hline 10\end{array}$ $\begin{array}{r}8\\+0\\\hline 8\end{array}$

Answer Key

Page 5

Addition

Name _____

Skill: Addition With Sums Through 10

Total Problems __35__

Problems Correct _____

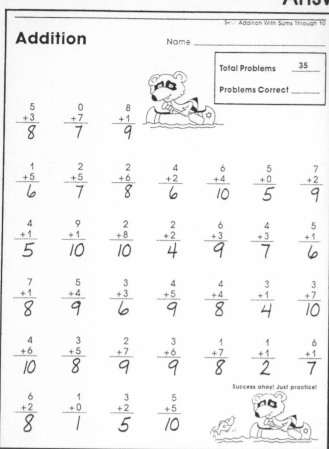

$5+3=8$ $0+7=7$ $8+1=9$

$1+5=6$ $2+5=7$ $2+6=8$ $4+2=6$ $6+4=10$ $5+0=5$ $7+2=9$

$4+1=5$ $9+1=10$ $2+8=10$ $2+2=4$ $6+3=9$ $4+3=7$ $5+1=6$

$7+1=8$ $5+4=9$ $3+3=6$ $4+5=9$ $4+4=8$ $3+1=4$ $3+7=10$

$4+6=10$ $3+5=8$ $2+7=9$ $3+6=9$ $1+7=8$ $1+1=2$ $6+1=7$

$6+2=8$ $1+0=1$ $3+2=5$ $5+5=10$

Success ahoy! Just practice!

Page 6

Addition

Name _____

Skill: Addition With Sums Through 10

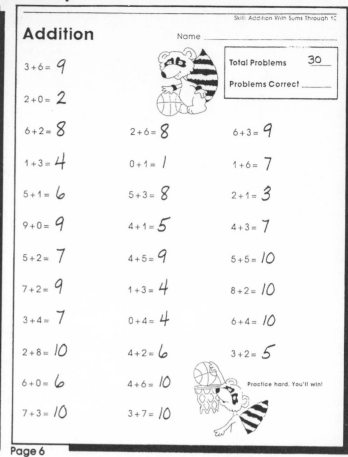

Total Problems __30__

Problems Correct _____

$3+6=9$
$2+0=2$
$6+2=8$ $2+6=8$ $6+3=9$
$1+3=4$ $0+1=1$ $1+6=7$
$5+1=6$ $5+3=8$ $2+1=3$
$9+0=9$ $4+1=5$ $4+3=7$
$5+2=7$ $4+5=9$ $5+5=10$
$7+2=9$ $1+3=4$ $8+2=10$
$3+4=7$ $0+4=4$ $6+4=10$
$2+8=10$ $4+2=6$ $3+2=5$
$6+0=6$ $4+6=10$
$7+3=10$ $3+7=10$

Practice hard. You'll win!

Page 7

Addition

Name _____

Skill: Addition With Sums Through 11

Total Problems __25__

Problems Correct _____

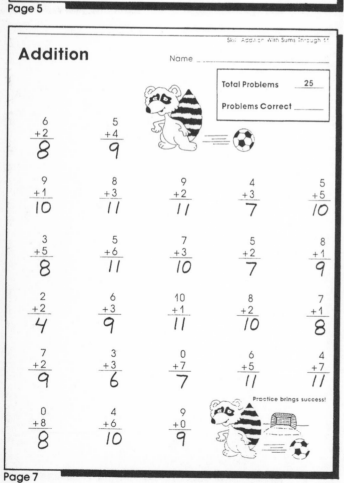

$6+2=8$ $5+4=9$

$9+1=10$ $8+3=11$ $9+2=11$ $4+3=7$ $5+5=10$

$3+5=8$ $5+6=11$ $7+3=10$ $5+2=7$ $8+1=9$

$2+2=4$ $6+3=9$ $10+1=11$ $8+2=10$ $7+1=8$

$7+2=9$ $3+3=6$ $0+7=7$ $6+5=11$ $4+7=11$

$0+8=8$ $4+6=10$ $9+0=9$

Practice brings success!

Page 8

Addition

Name _____

Skill: Addition With Sums Through 11

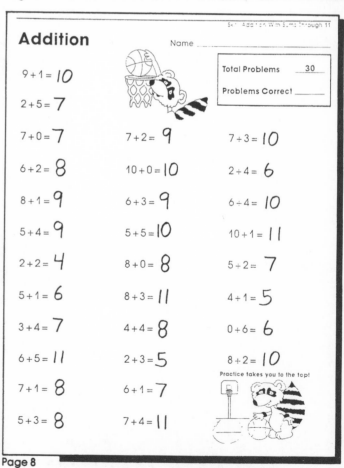

Total Problems __30__

Problems Correct _____

$9+1=10$
$2+5=7$
$7+0=7$ $7+2=9$ $7+3=10$
$6+2=8$ $10+0=10$ $2+4=6$
$8+1=9$ $6+3=9$ $6+4=10$
$5+4=9$ $5+5=10$ $10+1=11$
$2+2=4$ $8+0=8$ $5+2=7$
$5+1=6$ $8+3=11$ $4+1=5$
$3+4=7$ $4+4=8$ $0+6=6$
$6+5=11$ $2+3=5$ $8+2=10$
$7+1=8$ $6+1=7$
$5+3=8$ $7+4=11$

Practice takes you to the top!

Answer Key

Addition

Name _____

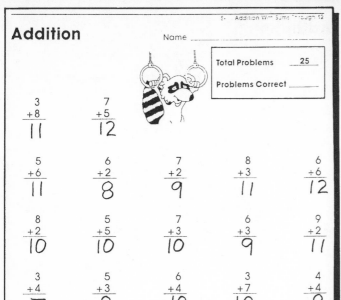

Total Problems ___25___

Problems Correct _____

$$\begin{array}{r}3\\+8\\\hline 11\end{array}\qquad \begin{array}{r}7\\+5\\\hline 12\end{array}$$

$$\begin{array}{r}5\\+6\\\hline 11\end{array}\quad \begin{array}{r}6\\+2\\\hline 8\end{array}\quad \begin{array}{r}7\\+2\\\hline 9\end{array}\quad \begin{array}{r}8\\+3\\\hline 11\end{array}\quad \begin{array}{r}6\\+6\\\hline 12\end{array}$$

$$\begin{array}{r}8\\+2\\\hline 10\end{array}\quad \begin{array}{r}5\\+5\\\hline 10\end{array}\quad \begin{array}{r}7\\+3\\\hline 10\end{array}\quad \begin{array}{r}6\\+3\\\hline 9\end{array}\quad \begin{array}{r}9\\+2\\\hline 11\end{array}$$

$$\begin{array}{r}3\\+4\\\hline 7\end{array}\quad \begin{array}{r}5\\+3\\\hline 8\end{array}\quad \begin{array}{r}6\\+4\\\hline 10\end{array}\quad \begin{array}{r}3\\+7\\\hline 10\end{array}\quad \begin{array}{r}4\\+4\\\hline 8\end{array}$$

$$\begin{array}{r}7\\+3\\\hline 10\end{array}\quad \begin{array}{r}9\\+0\\\hline 9\end{array}\quad \begin{array}{r}3\\+3\\\hline 6\end{array}\quad \begin{array}{r}8\\+4\\\hline 12\end{array}$$

Practice hard.
You'll win.

$$\begin{array}{r}9\\+1\\\hline 10\end{array}\quad \begin{array}{r}10\\+2\\\hline 12\end{array}\quad \begin{array}{r}5\\+4\\\hline 9\end{array}\quad \begin{array}{r}9\\+3\\\hline 12\end{array}$$

Addition

Name _____

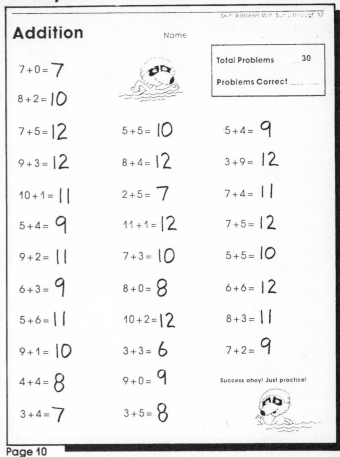

Total Problems ___30___

Problems Correct _____

$$7+0=7$$

$$8+2=10$$

$$7+5=12 \qquad 5+5=10 \qquad 5+4=9$$

$$9+3=12 \qquad 8+4=12 \qquad 3+9=12$$

$$10+1=11 \qquad 2+5=7 \qquad 7+4=11$$

$$5+4=9 \qquad 11+1=12 \qquad 7+5=12$$

$$9+2=11 \qquad 7+3=10 \qquad 5+5=10$$

$$6+3=9 \qquad 8+0=8 \qquad 6+6=12$$

$$5+6=11 \qquad 10+2=12 \qquad 8+3=11$$

$$9+1=10 \qquad 3+3=6 \qquad 7+2=9$$

$$4+4=8 \qquad 9+0=9$$

Success ahoy! Just practice!

$$3+4=7 \qquad 3+5=8$$

Addition

Name _____

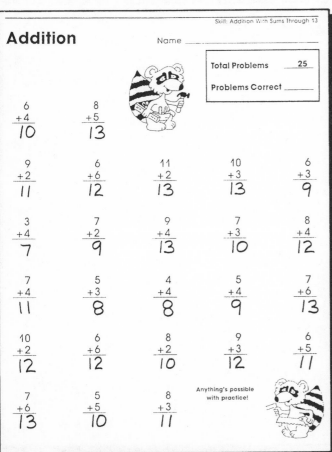

Total Problems ___25___

Problems Correct _____

$$\begin{array}{r}6\\+4\\\hline 10\end{array}\qquad \begin{array}{r}8\\+5\\\hline 13\end{array}$$

$$\begin{array}{r}9\\+2\\\hline 11\end{array}\quad \begin{array}{r}6\\+6\\\hline 12\end{array}\quad \begin{array}{r}11\\+2\\\hline 13\end{array}\quad \begin{array}{r}10\\+3\\\hline 13\end{array}\quad \begin{array}{r}6\\+3\\\hline 9\end{array}$$

$$\begin{array}{r}3\\+4\\\hline 7\end{array}\quad \begin{array}{r}7\\+2\\\hline 9\end{array}\quad \begin{array}{r}9\\+4\\\hline 13\end{array}\quad \begin{array}{r}7\\+3\\\hline 10\end{array}\quad \begin{array}{r}8\\+4\\\hline 12\end{array}$$

$$\begin{array}{r}7\\+4\\\hline 11\end{array}\quad \begin{array}{r}5\\+3\\\hline 8\end{array}\quad \begin{array}{r}4\\+4\\\hline 8\end{array}\quad \begin{array}{r}5\\+4\\\hline 9\end{array}\quad \begin{array}{r}7\\+6\\\hline 13\end{array}$$

$$\begin{array}{r}10\\+2\\\hline 12\end{array}\quad \begin{array}{r}6\\+6\\\hline 12\end{array}\quad \begin{array}{r}8\\+2\\\hline 10\end{array}\quad \begin{array}{r}9\\+3\\\hline 12\end{array}\quad \begin{array}{r}6\\+5\\\hline 11\end{array}$$

Anything's possible
with practice!

$$\begin{array}{r}7\\+6\\\hline 13\end{array}\quad \begin{array}{r}5\\+5\\\hline 10\end{array}\quad \begin{array}{r}8\\+3\\\hline 11\end{array}$$

Addition

Name _____

Total Problems ___25___

Problems Correct _____

$$\begin{array}{r}7\\+5\\\hline 12\end{array}\qquad \begin{array}{r}9\\+5\\\hline 14\end{array}$$

$$\begin{array}{r}6\\+5\\\hline 11\end{array}\quad \begin{array}{r}7\\+7\\\hline 14\end{array}\quad \begin{array}{r}8\\+5\\\hline 13\end{array}\quad \begin{array}{r}6\\+6\\\hline 12\end{array}\quad \begin{array}{r}9\\+4\\\hline 13\end{array}$$

$$\begin{array}{r}9\\+2\\\hline 11\end{array}\quad \begin{array}{r}6\\+4\\\hline 10\end{array}\quad \begin{array}{r}8\\+6\\\hline 14\end{array}\quad \begin{array}{r}7\\+4\\\hline 11\end{array}\quad \begin{array}{r}9\\+1\\\hline 10\end{array}$$

$$\begin{array}{r}8\\+3\\\hline 11\end{array}\quad \begin{array}{r}10\\+4\\\hline 14\end{array}\quad \begin{array}{r}3\\+7\\\hline 10\end{array}\quad \begin{array}{r}5\\+5\\\hline 10\end{array}\quad \begin{array}{r}6\\+8\\\hline 14\end{array}$$

$$\begin{array}{r}9\\+3\\\hline 12\end{array}\quad \begin{array}{r}5\\+2\\\hline 7\end{array}\quad \begin{array}{r}7\\+6\\\hline 13\end{array}\quad \begin{array}{r}5\\+9\\\hline 14\end{array}\quad \begin{array}{r}4\\+5\\\hline 9\end{array}$$

$$\begin{array}{r}6\\+3\\\hline 9\end{array}\quad \begin{array}{r}4\\+9\\\hline 13\end{array}\quad \begin{array}{r}3\\+4\\\hline 7\end{array}$$

Answer Key

Page 13

Addition   Name _____

Total Problems **30**

Problems Correct _____

$6+7=13$ $5+5=10$

$2+9=11$ $3+8=11$ $9+5=14$ $4+7=11$ $8+4=12$ $8+3=11$

$8+5=13$ $1+9=10$ $7+5=12$ $8+6=14$ $9+3=12$ $5+6=11$

$4+9=13$ $6+5=11$ $7+3=10$ $3+9=12$ $8+5=13$ $4+8=12$

$5+8=13$ $7+7=14$ $8+2=10$ $9+4=13$ $6+8=14$ $4+6=10$

$6+6=12$ $5+7=12$ $5+9=14$ $7+6=13$

Practice hard. You'll win.

Page 13

Page 14

Addition   Name _____

Total Problems **30**

Problems Correct _____

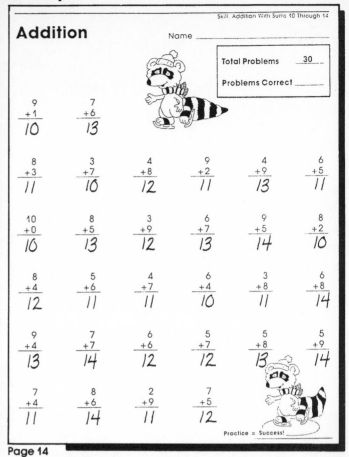

$9+1=10$ $7+6=13$

$8+3=11$ $3+7=10$ $4+8=12$ $9+2=11$ $4+9=13$ $6+5=11$

$10+0=10$ $8+5=13$ $3+9=12$ $6+7=13$ $9+5=14$ $8+2=10$

$8+4=12$ $5+6=11$ $4+7=11$ $6+4=10$ $3+8=11$ $6+8=14$

$9+4=13$ $7+7=14$ $6+6=12$ $5+7=12$ $5+8=13$ $5+9=14$

$7+4=11$ $8+6=14$ $2+9=11$ $7+5=12$

Practice = Success!

Page 14

Page 15

Addition   Name _____

Total Problems **30**

Problems Correct _____

$3+7=10$

$5+6=11$

$2+9=11$ $6+7=13$ $8+4=12$

$6+6=12$ $9+2=11$ $4+7=11$

$4+6=10$ $4+9=13$ $1+9=10$

$3+8=11$ $5+8=13$ $7+6=13$

$6+8=14$ $2+8=10$ $7+5=12$

$7+3=10$ $7+7=14$ $9+3=12$

$7+4=11$ $4+8=12$ $6+5=11$

$9+4=13$ $5+9=14$ $8+6=14$

$3+9=12$ $9+5=14$

$8+5=13$ $8+3=11$

Practice puts you on top!

Page 15

Page 16

Addition   Name _____

Total Problems **25**

Problems Correct _____

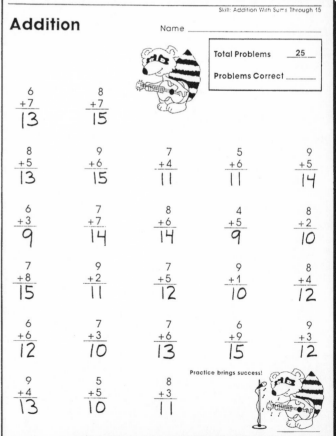

$6+7=13$ $8+7=15$

$8+5=13$ $9+6=15$ $7+4=11$ $5+6=11$ $9+5=14$

$6+3=9$ $7+7=14$ $8+6=14$ $4+5=9$ $8+2=10$

$7+8=15$ $9+2=11$ $7+5=12$ $9+1=10$ $8+4=12$

$6+6=12$ $7+3=10$ $7+6=13$ $6+9=15$ $9+3=12$

$9+4=13$ $5+5=10$ $8+3=11$

Practice brings success!

Page 16

Answer Key

Addition

Name _____

Total Problems ___25___

Problems Correct _____

$7+8=15$ $8+8=16$

$8+5=13$ $9+7=16$ $7+6=13$ $6+5=11$ $7+7=14$

$5+5=10$ $9+3=12$ $6+7=13$ $8+3=11$ $7+2=9$

$9+6=15$ $6+4=10$ $3+9=12$ $7+6=13$ $9+4=13$

$7+3=10$ $8+4=12$ $6+6=12$ $9+5=14$ $6+2=8$

$7+5=12$ $9+2=11$ $8+2=10$

Practice! Practice! Practice!

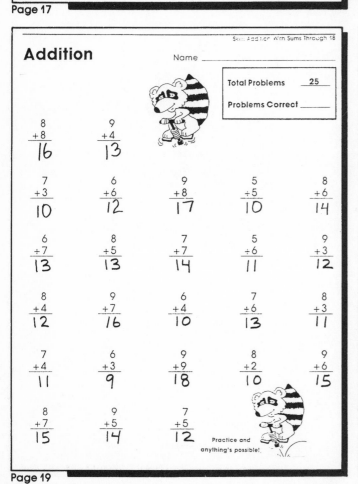

Page 17

Addition

Name _____

Total Problems ___25___

Problems Correct _____

$7+8=15$ $8+9=17$

$9+6=15$ $7+7=14$ $8+5=13$ $6+5=11$ $9+3=12$

$8+4=12$ $7+6=13$ $9+8=17$ $6+6=12$ $8+2=10$

$5+6=11$ $6+4=10$ $8+8=16$ $9+2=11$ $8+7=15$

$9+4=13$ $5+5=10$ $7+5=12$ $8+6=14$ $7+4=11$

$7+3=10$ $9+1=10$ $8+6=14$

Practice hard.   You'll win!

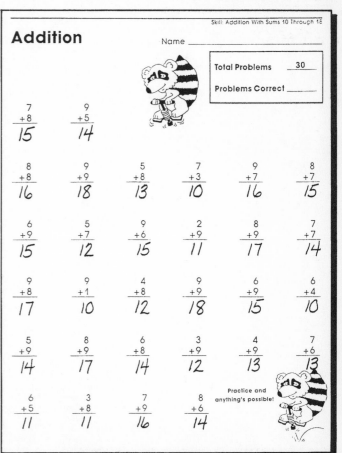

Page 18

Addition

Name _____

Total Problems ___25___

Problems Correct _____

$8+8=16$ $9+4=13$

$7+3=10$ $6+6=12$ $9+8=17$ $5+5=10$ $8+6=14$

$6+7=13$ $8+5=13$ $7+7=14$ $5+6=11$ $9+3=12$

$8+4=12$ $9+7=16$ $6+4=10$ $7+6=13$ $8+3=11$

$7+4=11$ $6+3=9$ $9+9=18$ $8+2=10$ $9+6=15$

$8+7=15$ $9+5=14$ $7+5=12$

Practice and anything's possible!

Page 19

Addition

Name _____

Total Problems ___30___

Problems Correct _____

$7+8=15$ $9+5=14$

$8+8=16$ $9+9=18$ $5+8=13$ $7+3=10$ $9+7=16$ $8+7=15$

$6+9=15$ $5+7=12$ $9+6=15$ $2+9=11$ $8+9=17$ $7+7=14$

$9+8=17$ $9+1=10$ $4+8=12$ $9+9=18$ $6+9=15$ $6+4=10$

$5+9=14$ $8+9=17$ $6+8=14$ $3+9=12$ $4+9=13$ $7+6=13$

$6+5=11$ $3+8=11$ $7+9=16$ $8+6=14$

Practice and anything's possible!

Page 20

Math IF8739   107

Answer Key

Addition

Name _____

Total Problems   30

Problems Correct _____

$9 + 4 = 13$ $6 + 6 = 12$

$8 + 7 = 15$ $2 + 9 = 11$ $9 + 9 = 18$ $5 + 5 = 10$ $7 + 6 = 13$ $8 + 9 = 17$

$7 + 4 = 11$ $6 + 4 = 10$ $9 + 8 = 17$ $8 + 3 = 11$ $8 + 8 = 16$ $7 + 5 = 12$

$5 + 8 = 13$ $6 + 8 = 14$ $7 + 9 = 16$ $9 + 6 = 15$ $5 + 9 = 14$ $6 + 7 = 13$

$5 + 6 = 11$ $7 + 8 = 15$ $6 + 9 = 15$ $8 + 6 = 14$ $2 + 8 = 10$ $7 + 7 = 14$

$1 + 9 = 10$ $9 + 7 = 16$ $8 + 4 = 12$ $3 + 9 = 12$

Practice hard.
You'll win!

Page 21

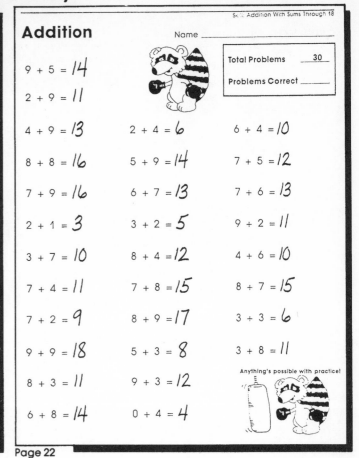

Addition

Name _____

Total Problems   30

Problems Correct _____

$9 + 5 = 14$

$2 + 9 = 11$

$4 + 9 = 13$ $2 + 4 = 6$ $6 + 4 = 10$

$8 + 8 = 16$ $5 + 9 = 14$ $7 + 5 = 12$

$7 + 9 = 16$ $6 + 7 = 13$ $7 + 6 = 13$

$2 + 1 = 3$ $3 + 2 = 5$ $9 + 2 = 11$

$3 + 7 = 10$ $8 + 4 = 12$ $4 + 6 = 10$

$7 + 4 = 11$ $7 + 8 = 15$ $8 + 7 = 15$

$7 + 2 = 9$ $8 + 9 = 17$ $3 + 3 = 6$

$9 + 9 = 18$ $5 + 3 = 8$ $3 + 8 = 11$

$8 + 3 = 11$ $9 + 3 = 12$

$6 + 8 = 14$ $0 + 4 = 4$

Anything's possible with practice!

Page 22

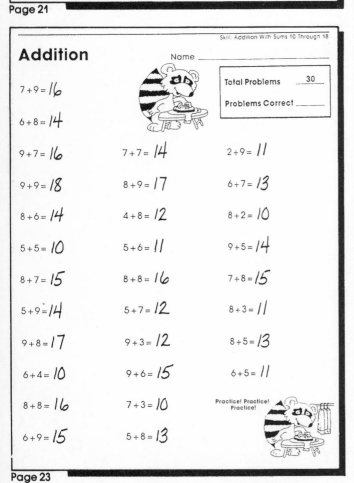

Addition

Name _____

Total Problems   30

Problems Correct _____

$7 + 9 = 16$

$6 + 8 = 14$

$9 + 7 = 16$ $7 + 7 = 14$ $2 + 9 = 11$

$9 + 9 = 18$ $8 + 9 = 17$ $6 + 7 = 13$

$8 + 6 = 14$ $4 + 8 = 12$ $8 + 2 = 10$

$5 + 5 = 10$ $5 + 6 = 11$ $9 + 5 = 14$

$8 + 7 = 15$ $8 + 8 = 16$ $7 + 8 = 15$

$5 + 9 = 14$ $5 + 7 = 12$ $8 + 3 = 11$

$9 + 8 = 17$ $9 + 3 = 12$ $8 + 5 = 13$

$6 + 4 = 10$ $9 + 6 = 15$ $6 + 5 = 11$

$8 + 8 = 16$ $7 + 3 = 10$

$6 + 9 = 15$ $5 + 8 = 13$

Practice! Practice!
Practice!

Page 23

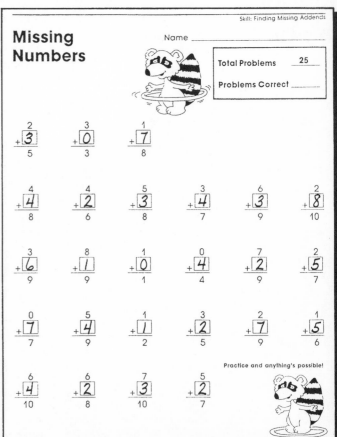

Missing Numbers

Name _____

Total Problems   25

Problems Correct _____

$2 + \boxed{3} = 5$ $3 + \boxed{0} = 3$ $1 + \boxed{7} = 8$

$\boxed{4} + 4 = 8$ $\boxed{4} + 2 = 6$ $5 + \boxed{3} = 8$ $3 + \boxed{4} = 7$ $6 + \boxed{3} = 9$ $2 + \boxed{8} = 10$

$3 + \boxed{6} = 9$ $8 + \boxed{1} = 9$ $1 + \boxed{0} = 1$ $0 + \boxed{4} = 4$ $7 + \boxed{2} = 9$ $2 + \boxed{5} = 7$

$0 + \boxed{7} = 7$ $5 + \boxed{4} = 9$ $1 + \boxed{1} = 2$ $3 + \boxed{2} = 5$ $2 + \boxed{7} = 9$ $1 + \boxed{5} = 6$

$6 + \boxed{4} = 10$ $6 + \boxed{2} = 8$ $7 + \boxed{3} = 10$ $5 + \boxed{2} = 7$

Practice and anything's possible!

Page 24

Answer Key

Page 25

Missing Numbers

Skill: Finding Missing Addends

Name _____

Total Problems	25
Problems Correct	_____

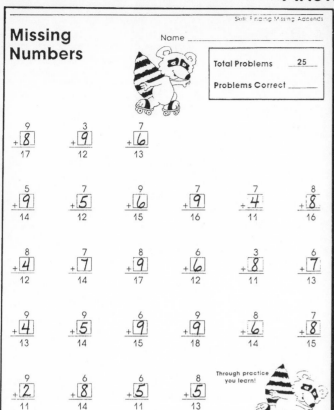

$9 + \boxed{8} = 17$ $3 + \boxed{9} = 12$ $7 + \boxed{6} = 13$

$5 + \boxed{9} = 14$ $7 + \boxed{5} = 12$ $9 + \boxed{6} = 15$ $7 + \boxed{9} = 16$ $7 + \boxed{4} = 11$ $8 + \boxed{8} = 16$

$8 + \boxed{4} = 12$ $7 + \boxed{7} = 14$ $8 + \boxed{9} = 17$ $6 + \boxed{6} = 12$ $3 + \boxed{8} = 11$ $6 + \boxed{7} = 13$

$9 + \boxed{4} = 13$ $9 + \boxed{5} = 14$ $6 + \boxed{9} = 15$ $9 + \boxed{9} = 18$ $8 + \boxed{6} = 14$ $7 + \boxed{8} = 15$

$9 + \boxed{2} = 11$ $6 + \boxed{8} = 14$ $6 + \boxed{5} = 11$ $8 + \boxed{5} = 13$

Through practice you learn!

Page 26

Missing Numbers

Skill: Finding Missing Addends

Name _____

Total Problems	25
Problems Correct	_____

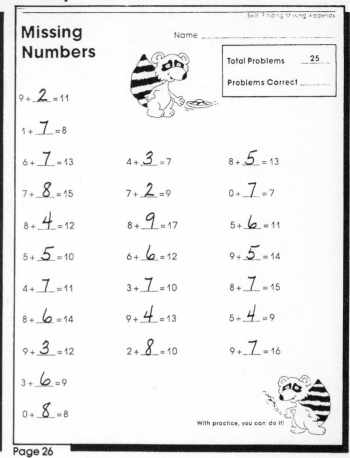

$9 + \boxed{2} = 11$

$1 + \boxed{7} = 8$

$6 + \boxed{7} = 13$ $4 + \boxed{3} = 7$ $8 + \boxed{5} = 13$

$7 + \boxed{8} = 15$ $7 + \boxed{2} = 9$ $0 + \boxed{7} = 7$

$8 + \boxed{4} = 12$ $8 + \boxed{9} = 17$ $5 + \boxed{6} = 11$

$5 + \boxed{5} = 10$ $6 + \boxed{6} = 12$ $9 + \boxed{5} = 14$

$4 + \boxed{7} = 11$ $3 + \boxed{7} = 10$ $8 + \boxed{7} = 15$

$8 + \boxed{6} = 14$ $9 + \boxed{4} = 13$ $5 + \boxed{4} = 9$

$9 + \boxed{3} = 12$ $2 + \boxed{8} = 10$ $9 + \boxed{7} = 16$

$3 + \boxed{6} = 9$

$0 + \boxed{8} = 8$

With practice, you can do it!

Page 27

Addition

Skill: Addition With Three Addends With Sums Through 6

Name _____

Total Problems	25
Problems Correct	_____

2 1 +2 = **5**	3 0 +1 = **4**			
1 1 +1 = **3**	2 1 +3 = **6**	0 2 +2 = **4**	2 0 +1 = **3**	1 3 +0 = **4**
3 1 +2 = **6**	2 1 +0 = **3**	1 2 +1 = **4**	2 1 +0 = **3**	5 1 +0 = **6**
4 0 +1 = **5**	2 3 +1 = **6**	2 0 +4 = **6**	3 1 +0 = **4**	0 5 +1 = **6**
2 1 +2 = **5**	5 0 +1 = **6**	3 0 +2 = **5**	4 1 +1 = **6**	0 3 +1 = **4**
2 1 +0 = **3**	3 2 +1 = **6**	0 4 +1 = **5**		

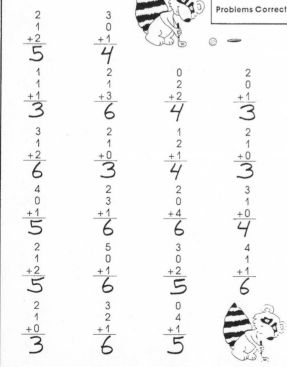

Page 28

Addition

Skill: Addition With 3 Addends With Sums Through 6

Name _____

Total Problems	30
Problems Correct	_____

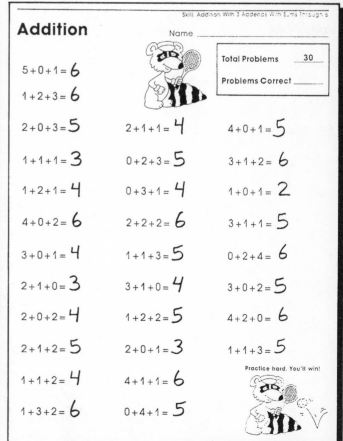

$5 + 0 + 1 = 6$

$1 + 2 + 3 = 6$

$2 + 0 + 3 = 5$ $2 + 1 + 1 = 4$ $4 + 0 + 1 = 5$

$1 + 1 + 1 = 3$ $0 + 2 + 3 = 5$ $3 + 1 + 2 = 6$

$1 + 2 + 1 = 4$ $0 + 3 + 1 = 4$ $1 + 0 + 1 = 2$

$4 + 0 + 2 = 6$ $2 + 2 + 2 = 6$ $3 + 1 + 1 = 5$

$3 + 0 + 1 = 4$ $1 + 1 + 3 = 5$ $0 + 2 + 4 = 6$

$2 + 1 + 0 = 3$ $3 + 1 + 0 = 4$ $3 + 0 + 2 = 5$

$2 + 0 + 2 = 4$ $1 + 2 + 2 = 5$ $4 + 2 + 0 = 6$

$2 + 1 + 2 = 5$ $2 + 0 + 1 = 3$ $1 + 1 + 3 = 5$

$1 + 1 + 2 = 4$ $4 + 1 + 1 = 6$

$1 + 3 + 2 = 6$ $0 + 4 + 1 = 5$

Practice hard. You'll win!

Answer Key

Page 29

Addition

Name _____

Total Problems ___25___
Problems Correct _____

```
  3      5
  0      1
 +4     +2
 ──     ──
  7      8
```

```
  6      4      2      5      4
  0      2      3      1      3
 +4     +2     +1     +2     +2
 ──     ──     ──     ──     ──
 10      8      6      8      9
```

```
  2      3      8      3      7
  5      0      0      3      1
 +2     +4     +1     +4     +2
 ──     ──     ──     ──     ──
  9      7      9     10     10
```

```
  5      2      6      3      8
  2      2      2      2      0
 +1     +2     +1     +3     +1
 ──     ──     ──     ──     ──
  8      6      9      8      9
```

```
  2      6      2      7      5
  2      1      3      2      1
 +4     +0     +4     +1     +2
 ──     ──     ──     ──     ──
  8      7      9     10      8
```

```
  6      0      3
  3      4      3
 +1     +2     +3
 ──     ──     ──
 10      6      9
```

Practice! Practice! Practice!

Page 30

Addition

Name _____

Total Problems ___30___
Problems Correct _____

$7+2+1=10$

$3+0+4=7$

$5+2+3=10$	$3+3+2=8$	$5+3+1=9$
$6+1+2=9$	$5+4+1=10$	$2+3+2=7$
$2+4+1=7$	$6+2+0=8$	$4+2+3=9$
$3+3+3=9$	$4+0+2=6$	$8+1+0=9$
$6+0+1=7$	$6+1+0=7$	$2+0+3=5$
$4+2+2=8$	$2+2+2=6$	$6+3+1=10$
$5+2+1=8$	$3+4+1=8$	$3+0+3=6$
$7+0+2=9$	$1+2+1=4$	$5+1+1=7$
$2+2+6=10$	$6+3+1=10$	
$5+1+3=9$	$7+0+1=8$	

Success ahoy! Just practice!

Page 31

Addition

Name _____

Total Problems ___25___
Problems Correct _____

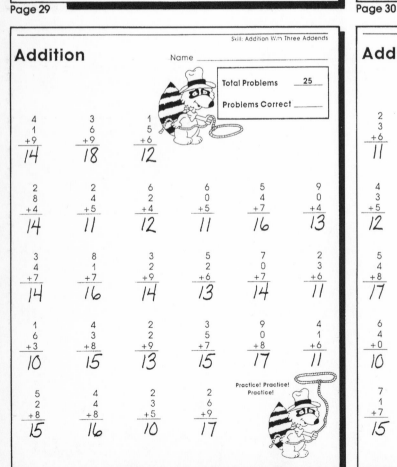

```
  4      3      1
  1      6      5
 +9     +9     +6
 ──     ──     ──
 14     18     12
```

```
  2      2      6      6      5      9
  8      4      2      0      4      0
 +4     +5     +4     +5     +7     +4
 ──     ──     ──     ──     ──     ──
 14     11     12     11     16     13
```

```
  3      8      3      5      7      2
  4      1      2      2      0      3
 +7     +7     +9     +6     +7     +6
 ──     ──     ──     ──     ──     ──
 14     16     14     13     14     11
```

```
  1      4      2      3      9      4
  6      3      2      5      0      1
 +3     +8     +9     +7     +8     +6
 ──     ──     ──     ──     ──     ──
 10     15     13     15     17     11
```

```
  5      4      2      2
  2      4      3      6
 +8     +8     +5     +9
 ──     ──     ──     ──
 15     16     10     17
```

Practice! Practice! Practice!

Page 32

Addition

Name _____

Total Problems ___25___
Problems Correct _____

```
  2      1      5
  3      0      2
 +6     +8     +6
 ──     ──     ──
 11      9     13
```

```
  4      8      6      2      3      2
  3      0      3      3      3      2
 +5     +3     +5     +9     +9     +6
 ──     ──     ──     ──     ──     ──
 12     11     14     14     15     10
```

```
  5      7      1      4      4      3
  4      2      3      2      5      5
 +8     +8     +8     +8     +7     +7
 ──     ──     ──     ──     ──     ──
 17     17     12     14     16     15
```

```
  6      2      6      4      5      5
  4      4      2      4      1      5
 +0     +5     +6     +8     +7     +1
 ──     ──     ──     ──     ──     ──
 10     11     14     16     13     11
```

```
  7      8      9      1
  1      1      1      5
 +7     +9     +5     +6
 ──     ──     ──     ──
 15     18     15     12
```

Practice = Success!

Answer Key

Page 33

Addition

Name _____

Total Problems ___25___

Problems Correct _____

55 +32 = 87	47 +21 = 68			
37 +51 = 88	65 +34 = 99	44 +32 = 76	62 +34 = 96	14 +42 = 56
75 +24 = 99	36 +41 = 77	16 +60 = 76	25 +53 = 78	52 +42 = 94
23 +14 = 37	43 +25 = 68	28 +51 = 79	37 +30 = 67	61 +26 = 87
42 +51 = 93	30 +48 = 78	37 +22 = 59	55 +22 = 77	46 +30 = 76
60 +18 = 78	15 +13 = 28	70 +11 = 81		

Practice hard. You'll win.

Page 33

Page 34

Addition

Name _____

Total Problems ___25___

Problems Correct _____

61 +27 = 88	24 +24 = 48			
14 +24 = 38	23 +52 = 75	40 +40 = 80	60 +20 = 80	46 +53 = 99
24 +35 = 59	35 +34 = 69	30 +40 = 70	21 +52 = 73	70 +18 = 88
45 +30 = 75	34 +12 = 46	72 +14 = 86	35 +13 = 48	24 +43 = 67
25 +61 = 86	42 +17 = 59	53 +23 = 76	10 +50 = 60	24 +44 = 68
52 +20 = 72	33 +14 = 47	54 +13 = 67		

With practice, you can do it!

Page 34

Page 35

Addition

Name _____

Total Problems ___25___

Problems Correct _____

95 +33 = 128	94 +93 = 187			
71 +71 = 142	27 +82 = 109	94 +64 = 158	71 +66 = 137	85 +91 = 176
74 +95 = 169	33 +85 = 118	44 +92 = 136	82 +71 = 153	52 +85 = 137
93 +26 = 119	60 +85 = 145	53 +72 = 125	41 +75 = 116	32 +72 = 104
95 +44 = 139	52 +56 = 108	80 +60 = 140	92 +54 = 146	83 +84 = 167
97 +81 = 178	43 +83 = 126	74 +80 = 154		

With practice, you can do it!

Page 35

Page 36

Addition

Name _____

Total Problems ___25___

Problems Correct _____

47 +51 = 98	30 +20 = 50			
64 +32 = 96	32 +27 = 59	56 +20 = 76	43 +25 = 68	15 +10 = 25
54 +13 = 67	24 +15 = 39	35 +42 = 77	11 +62 = 73	12 +12 = 24
23 +62 = 85	20 +71 = 91	16 +42 = 58	12 +15 = 27	51 +25 = 76
21 +16 = 37	31 +13 = 44	42 +20 = 62	70 +10 = 80	27 +32 = 59
76 +23 = 99	55 +14 = 69	52 +33 = 85		

Through practice you learn!

Page 36

Answer Key

Page 37

Addition

Name _____

Total Problems ___25___

Problems Correct _____

25 + 32 = **57**	72 + 17 = **89**			
81 + 10 = **91**	62 + 36 = **98**	11 + 18 = **29**	44 + 23 = **67**	42 + 21 = **63**
61 + 26 = **87**	35 + 43 = **78**	10 + 60 = **70**	19 + 20 = **39**	23 + 53 = **76**
14 + 41 = **55**	45 + 14 = **59**	33 + 42 = **75**	28 + 61 = **89**	60 + 34 = **94**
37 + 22 = **59**	41 + 41 = **82**	12 + 21 = **33**	14 + 54 = **68**	24 + 72 = **96**
15 + 11 = **26**	63 + 21 = **84**	21 + 25 = **46**		

Practice and anything's possible!

Page 37

Page 38

Addition

Name _____

Total Problems ___25___

Problems Correct _____

72 + 22 = **94**	17 + 37 = **54**			
16 + 15 = **31**	49 + 11 = **60**	56 + 19 = **75**	32 + 47 = **79**	20 + 16 = **36**
36 + 17 = **53**	57 + 39 = **96**	24 + 44 = **68**	68 + 25 = **93**	39 + 39 = **78**
49 + 24 = **73**	55 + 33 = **88**	29 + 28 = **57**	48 + 17 = **65**	23 + 14 = **37**
36 + 45 = **81**	12 + 58 = **70**	28 + 24 = **52**	21 + 22 = **43**	19 + 67 = **86**
47 + 35 = **82**	27 + 18 = **45**	52 + 43 = **95**		

Practice brings success!

Page 38

Page 39

Addition

Name _____

Total Problems ___25___

Problems Correct _____

15 + 16 = **31**	29 + 33 = **62**			
38 + 28 = **66**	56 + 26 = **82**	17 + 60 = **77**	19 + 16 = **35**	40 + 17 = **57**
35 + 15 = **50**	31 + 58 = **89**	36 + 18 = **54**	45 + 39 = **84**	13 + 28 = **41**
63 + 23 = **86**	26 + 27 = **53**	49 + 39 = **88**	22 + 43 = **65**	30 + 40 = **70**
53 + 46 = **99**	16 + 58 = **74**	81 + 12 = **93**	38 + 29 = **67**	42 + 38 = **80**
77 + 13 = **90**	19 + 18 = **37**	54 + 25 = **79**		

Anything's possible with practice!

Page 39

Page 40

Addition

Name _____

Total Problems ___25___

Problems Correct _____

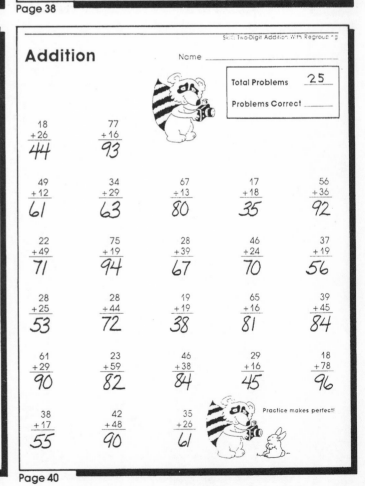

18 + 26 = **44**	77 + 16 = **93**			
49 + 12 = **61**	34 + 29 = **63**	67 + 13 = **80**	17 + 18 = **35**	56 + 36 = **92**
22 + 49 = **71**	75 + 19 = **94**	28 + 39 = **67**	46 + 24 = **70**	37 + 19 = **56**
28 + 25 = **53**	28 + 44 = **72**	19 + 19 = **38**	65 + 16 = **81**	39 + 45 = **84**
61 + 29 = **90**	23 + 59 = **82**	46 + 38 = **84**	29 + 16 = **45**	18 + 78 = **96**
38 + 17 = **55**	42 + 48 = **90**	35 + 26 = **61**		

Practice makes perfect!

Page 40

© 1990 Instructional Fair, Inc.

Answer Key

Page 41

Addition

Skill: Two-Digit Addition With Regrouping

Name _____

Total Problems ___25___

Problems Correct _____

$38 + 12 = 50$ $47 + 15 = 62$

$49 + 28 = 77$ $27 + 36 = 63$ $16 + 45 = 61$ $66 + 29 = 95$ $18 + 56 = 74$

$28 + 15 = 43$ $49 + 38 = 87$ $67 + 27 = 94$ $39 + 17 = 56$ $38 + 47 = 85$

$57 + 39 = 96$ $26 + 26 = 52$ $17 + 24 = 41$ $34 + 36 = 70$ $18 + 19 = 37$

$35 + 29 = 64$ $58 + 14 = 72$ $23 + 27 = 50$ $29 + 29 = 58$ $19 + 74 = 93$

$66 + 15 = 81$ $38 + 13 = 51$ $59 + 19 = 78$

Page 42

Addition

Skill: Two-Digit Addition With Regrouping

Name _____

Total Problems ___25___

Problems Correct _____

$55 + 37 = 92$ $13 + 28 = 41$

$44 + 38 = 82$ $48 + 27 = 75$ $37 + 17 = 54$ $78 + 19 = 97$ $15 + 28 = 43$

$66 + 27 = 93$ $42 + 29 = 71$ $21 + 39 = 60$ $65 + 26 = 91$ $38 + 36 = 74$

$22 + 18 = 40$ $27 + 19 = 46$ $26 + 59 = 85$ $29 + 23 = 52$ $18 + 18 = 36$

$39 + 38 = 77$ $16 + 16 = 32$ $67 + 18 = 85$ $14 + 49 = 63$ $24 + 56 = 80$

$34 + 37 = 71$ $49 + 39 = 88$ $45 + 19 = 64$

Practice puts you on top!

Page 43

Addition

Skill: Two- and Three-Digit Addition With No Regrouping

Name _____

Total Problems ___25___

Problems Correct _____

$522 + 344 = 866$ $124 + 50 = 174$

$26 + 60 = 86$ $53 + 26 = 79$ $608 + 201 = 809$ $171 + 16 = 187$ $200 + 300 = 500$

$376 + 103 = 479$ $701 + 217 = 918$ $43 + 20 = 63$ $330 + 150 = 480$ $141 + 121 = 262$

$800 + 53 = 853$ $164 + 14 = 178$ $135 + 221 = 356$ $918 + 60 = 978$ $70 + 20 = 90$

$12 + 33 = 45$ $640 + 35 = 675$ $252 + 32 = 284$ $461 + 327 = 788$ $445 + 53 = 498$

$112 + 205 = 317$ $251 + 740 = 991$ $232 + 344 = 576$

Page 44

Addition

Skill: Three-Digit Addition With No Regrouping

Name _____

Total Problems ___25___

Problems Correct _____

$284 + 513 = 797$ $534 + 225 = 759$

$625 + 243 = 868$ $130 + 160 = 290$ $472 + 227 = 699$ $242 + 314 = 556$ $120 + 345 = 465$

$391 + 408 = 799$ $423 + 152 = 575$ $112 + 203 = 315$ $362 + 322 = 684$ $513 + 373 = 886$

$303 + 104 = 407$ $421 + 221 = 642$ $661 + 235 = 896$ $231 + 212 = 443$ $710 + 213 = 923$

$446 + 152 = 598$ $212 + 162 = 374$ $531 + 432 = 963$ $320 + 131 = 451$ $255 + 432 = 687$

$234 + 304 = 538$ $300 + 200 = 500$ $191 + 101 = 292$

Answer Key

Page 45

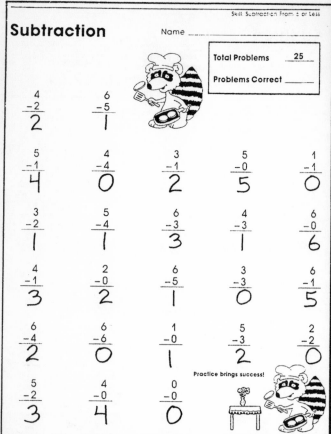

Subtraction

Name _____

Skill: Subtraction From 6 or Less

Total Problems   25

Problems Correct _____

4 − 2 = 2	6 − 5 = 1			
5 − 1 = 4	4 − 4 = 0	3 − 1 = 2	5 − 0 = 5	1 − 1 = 0
3 − 2 = 1	5 − 4 = 1	6 − 3 = 3	4 − 3 = 1	6 − 0 = 6
4 − 1 = 3	2 − 0 = 2	6 − 5 = 1	3 − 3 = 0	6 − 1 = 5
6 − 4 = 2	6 − 6 = 0	1 − 0 = 1	5 − 3 = 2	2 − 2 = 0
5 − 2 = 3	4 − 0 = 4	0 − 0 = 0		

Practice brings success!

Page 45

Page 46

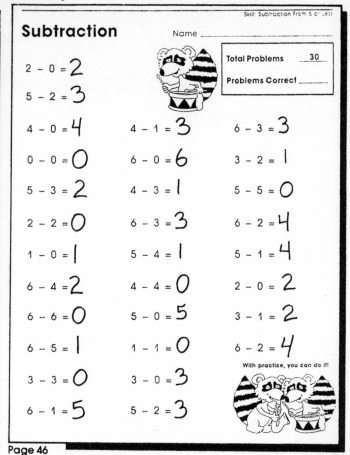

Subtraction

Name _____

Skill: Subtraction From 6 or Less

Total Problems   30

Problems Correct _____

2 − 0 = 2
5 − 2 = 3

4 − 0 = 4   4 − 1 = 3   6 − 3 = 3
0 − 0 = 0   6 − 0 = 6   3 − 2 = 1
5 − 3 = 2   4 − 3 = 1   5 − 5 = 0
2 − 2 = 0   6 − 3 = 3   6 − 2 = 4
1 − 0 = 1   5 − 4 = 1   5 − 1 = 4
6 − 4 = 2   4 − 4 = 0   2 − 0 = 2
6 − 6 = 0   5 − 0 = 5   3 − 1 = 2
6 − 5 = 1   1 − 1 = 0   6 − 2 = 4
3 − 3 = 0   3 − 0 = 3
6 − 1 = 5   5 − 2 = 3

With practice, you can do it!

Page 46

Page 47

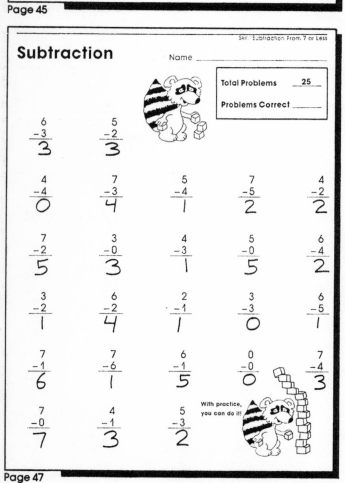

Subtraction

Name _____

Skill: Subtraction From 7 or Less

Total Problems   25

Problems Correct _____

6 − 3 = 3	5 − 2 = 3			
4 − 4 = 0	7 − 3 = 4	5 − 4 = 1	7 − 5 = 2	4 − 2 = 2
7 − 2 = 5	3 − 0 = 3	4 − 3 = 1	5 − 0 = 5	6 − 4 = 2
3 − 2 = 1	6 − 2 = 4	2 − 1 = 1	3 − 3 = 0	6 − 5 = 1
7 − 1 = 6	7 − 6 = 1	6 − 1 = 5	0 − 0 = 0	7 − 4 = 3
7 − 0 = 7	4 − 1 = 3	5 − 3 = 2		

With practice, you can do it!

Page 47

Page 48

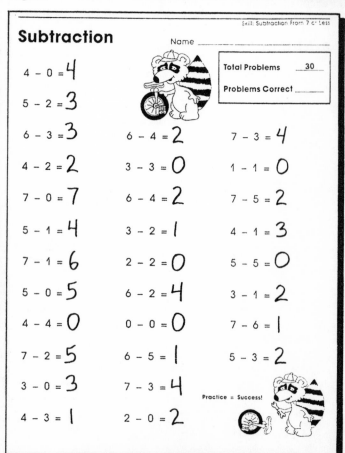

Subtraction

Name _____

Skill: Subtraction From 7 or Less

Total Problems   30

Problems Correct _____

4 − 0 = 4
5 − 2 = 3

6 − 3 = 3   6 − 4 = 2   7 − 3 = 4
4 − 2 = 2   3 − 3 = 0   1 − 1 = 0
7 − 0 = 7   6 − 4 = 2   7 − 5 = 2
5 − 1 = 4   3 − 2 = 1   4 − 1 = 3
7 − 1 = 6   2 − 2 = 0   5 − 5 = 0
5 − 0 = 5   6 − 2 = 4   3 − 1 = 2
4 − 4 = 0   0 − 0 = 0   7 − 6 = 1
7 − 2 = 5   6 − 5 = 1   5 − 3 = 2
3 − 0 = 3   7 − 3 = 4
4 − 3 = 1   2 − 0 = 2

Practice = Success!

Page 48

Answer Key

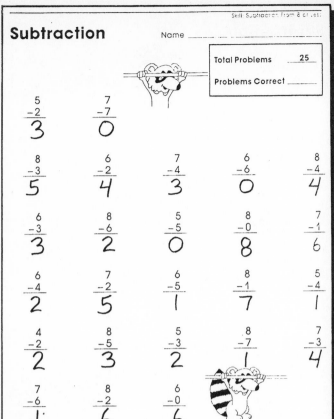

Subtraction

Name _____

Total Problems **25**

Problems Correct _____

$5 - 2 = 3$	$7 - 7 = 0$			
$8 - 3 = 5$	$6 - 2 = 4$	$7 - 4 = 3$	$6 - 6 = 0$	$8 - 4 = 4$
$6 - 3 = 3$	$8 - 6 = 2$	$5 - 5 = 0$	$8 - 0 = 8$	$7 - 1 = 6$
$6 - 4 = 2$	$7 - 2 = 5$	$6 - 5 = 1$	$8 - 1 = 7$	$5 - 4 = 1$
$4 - 2 = 2$	$8 - 5 = 3$	$5 - 3 = 2$	$8 - 7 = 1$	$7 - 3 = 4$
$7 - 6 = 1$	$8 - 2 = 6$	$6 - 0 = 6$		

Page 49

Subtraction

Name _____

Total Problems **30**

Problems Correct _____

$7 - 6 = 1$

$6 - 4 = 2$

$7 - 2 = 5$

$5 - 0 = 5$	$6 - 6 = 0$	$2 - 2 = 0$
$8 - 1 = 7$	$8 - 2 = 6$	$5 - 2 = 3$
$5 - 4 = 1$	$6 - 3 = 3$	$7 - 7 = 0$
$3 - 3 = 0$	$7 - 4 = 3$	$8 - 5 = 3$
$4 - 2 = 2$	$6 - 4 = 2$	$7 - 5 = 2$
$7 - 0 = 7$	$7 - 3 = 4$	$5 - 1 = 4$
$5 - 3 = 2$	$8 - 0 = 8$	$4 - 4 = 0$
$8 - 7 = 1$	$5 - 5 = 0$	$6 - 5 = 1$
$7 - 3 = 4$	$7 - 1 = 6$	
	$8 - 3 = 5$	

Practice and anything's possible!

Page 50

Subtraction

Name _____

Total Problems **25**

Problems Correct _____

$8 - 6 = 2$	$9 - 3 = 6$			
$7 - 5 = 2$	$8 - 8 = 0$	$9 - 4 = 5$	$5 - 3 = 2$	$8 - 2 = 6$
$9 - 0 = 9$	$7 - 2 = 5$	$8 - 3 = 5$	$9 - 6 = 3$	$7 - 4 = 3$
$9 - 5 = 4$	$5 - 4 = 1$	$9 - 1 = 8$	$7 - 3 = 4$	$6 - 2 = 4$
$8 - 1 = 7$	$6 - 5 = 1$	$9 - 2 = 7$	$7 - 1 = 6$	$8 - 4 = 4$
$9 - 9 = 0$	$8 - 5 = 3$	$7 - 6 = 1$		

Practice! Practice! Practice!

Page 51

Subtraction

Name _____

Total Problems **30**

Problems Correct _____

$9 - 3 = 6$

$7 - 2 = 5$

$9 - 0 = 9$	$5 - 4 = 1$	$6 - 6 = 0$
$8 - 3 = 5$	$9 - 5 = 4$	$8 - 0 = 8$
$9 - 6 = 3$	$7 - 3 = 4$	$7 - 6 = 1$
$7 - 4 = 3$	$9 - 1 = 8$	$8 - 4 = 4$
$8 - 2 = 6$	$6 - 2 = 4$	$7 - 1 = 6$
$5 - 3 = 2$	$4 - 4 = 0$	$6 - 3 = 3$
$9 - 4 = 5$	$7 - 0 = 7$	$7 - 7 = 0$
$8 - 8 = 0$	$8 - 1 = 7$	$8 - 6 = 2$
$7 - 5 = 2$	$6 - 5 = 1$	
$9 - 9 = 0$	$9 - 2 = 7$	

Practice and anything's possible!

Page 52

Answer Key

Subtraction

Name _____

Skill: Subtraction From 10 or Less

Total Problems	25
Problems Correct	___

$\begin{array}{r}7\\-5\\\hline 2\end{array}$	$\begin{array}{r}10\\-3\\\hline 7\end{array}$			
$\begin{array}{r}8\\-6\\\hline 2\end{array}$	$\begin{array}{r}10\\-4\\\hline 6\end{array}$	$\begin{array}{r}7\\-3\\\hline 4\end{array}$	$\begin{array}{r}9\\-6\\\hline 3\end{array}$	$\begin{array}{r}8\\-7\\\hline 1\end{array}$
$\begin{array}{r}10\\-5\\\hline 5\end{array}$	$\begin{array}{r}9\\-3\\\hline 6\end{array}$	$\begin{array}{r}8\\-7\\\hline 1\end{array}$	$\begin{array}{r}10\\-1\\\hline 9\end{array}$	$\begin{array}{r}9\\-6\\\hline 3\end{array}$
$\begin{array}{r}8\\-2\\\hline 6\end{array}$	$\begin{array}{r}9\\-5\\\hline 4\end{array}$	$\begin{array}{r}10\\-0\\\hline 10\end{array}$	$\begin{array}{r}7\\-6\\\hline 1\end{array}$	$\begin{array}{r}8\\-4\\\hline 4\end{array}$
$\begin{array}{r}7\\-2\\\hline 5\end{array}$	$\begin{array}{r}10\\-4\\\hline 6\end{array}$	$\begin{array}{r}9\\-4\\\hline 5\end{array}$	$\begin{array}{r}10\\-10\\\hline 0\end{array}$	$\begin{array}{r}7\\-4\\\hline 3\end{array}$
$\begin{array}{r}10\\-2\\\hline 8\end{array}$	$\begin{array}{r}6\\-2\\\hline 4\end{array}$	$\begin{array}{r}8\\-5\\\hline 3\end{array}$		

Anything's possible with practice!

Page 53

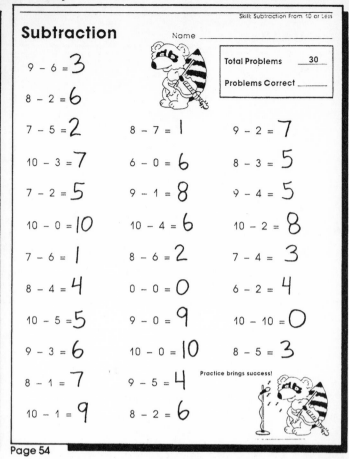

Subtraction

Name _____

Skill: Subtraction From 10 or Less

Total Problems	30
Problems Correct	___

$9 - 6 = 3$

$8 - 2 = 6$

$7 - 5 = 2$	$8 - 7 = 1$	$9 - 2 = 7$
$10 - 3 = 7$	$6 - 0 = 6$	$8 - 3 = 5$
$7 - 2 = 5$	$9 - 1 = 8$	$9 - 4 = 5$
$10 - 0 = 10$	$10 - 4 = 6$	$10 - 2 = 8$
$7 - 6 = 1$	$8 - 6 = 2$	$7 - 4 = 3$
$8 - 4 = 4$	$0 - 0 = 0$	$6 - 2 = 4$
$10 - 5 = 5$	$9 - 0 = 9$	$10 - 10 = 0$
$9 - 3 = 6$	$10 - 0 = 10$	$8 - 5 = 3$
$8 - 1 = 7$	$9 - 5 = 4$	
$10 - 1 = 9$	$8 - 2 = 6$	

Practice brings success!

Page 54

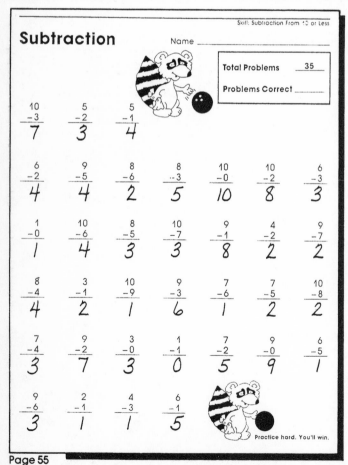

Subtraction

Name _____

Skill: Subtraction From 10 or Less

Total Problems	35
Problems Correct	___

$\begin{array}{r}10\\-3\\\hline 7\end{array}$	$\begin{array}{r}5\\-2\\\hline 3\end{array}$	$\begin{array}{r}5\\-1\\\hline 4\end{array}$				
$\begin{array}{r}6\\-2\\\hline 4\end{array}$	$\begin{array}{r}9\\-5\\\hline 4\end{array}$	$\begin{array}{r}8\\-6\\\hline 2\end{array}$	$\begin{array}{r}8\\-3\\\hline 5\end{array}$	$\begin{array}{r}10\\-0\\\hline 10\end{array}$	$\begin{array}{r}10\\-2\\\hline 8\end{array}$	$\begin{array}{r}6\\-3\\\hline 3\end{array}$
$\begin{array}{r}1\\-0\\\hline 1\end{array}$	$\begin{array}{r}10\\-6\\\hline 4\end{array}$	$\begin{array}{r}8\\-5\\\hline 3\end{array}$	$\begin{array}{r}10\\-7\\\hline 3\end{array}$	$\begin{array}{r}9\\-1\\\hline 8\end{array}$	$\begin{array}{r}4\\-2\\\hline 2\end{array}$	$\begin{array}{r}9\\-7\\\hline 2\end{array}$
$\begin{array}{r}8\\-4\\\hline 4\end{array}$	$\begin{array}{r}3\\-1\\\hline 2\end{array}$	$\begin{array}{r}10\\-9\\\hline 1\end{array}$	$\begin{array}{r}9\\-3\\\hline 6\end{array}$	$\begin{array}{r}7\\-6\\\hline 1\end{array}$	$\begin{array}{r}7\\-5\\\hline 2\end{array}$	$\begin{array}{r}10\\-8\\\hline 2\end{array}$
$\begin{array}{r}7\\-4\\\hline 3\end{array}$	$\begin{array}{r}9\\-2\\\hline 7\end{array}$	$\begin{array}{r}3\\-0\\\hline 3\end{array}$	$\begin{array}{r}1\\-1\\\hline 0\end{array}$	$\begin{array}{r}7\\-2\\\hline 5\end{array}$	$\begin{array}{r}9\\-0\\\hline 9\end{array}$	$\begin{array}{r}6\\-5\\\hline 1\end{array}$
$\begin{array}{r}9\\-6\\\hline 3\end{array}$	$\begin{array}{r}2\\-1\\\hline 1\end{array}$	$\begin{array}{r}4\\-3\\\hline 1\end{array}$	$\begin{array}{r}6\\-1\\\hline 5\end{array}$			

Practice hard. You'll win.

Page 55

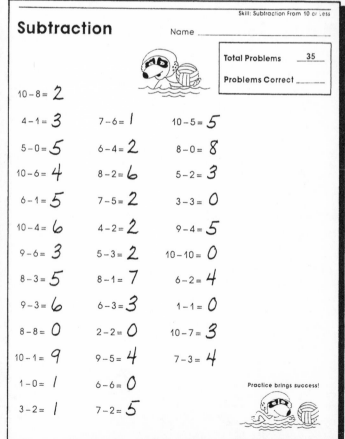

Subtraction

Name _____

Skill: Subtraction From 10 or Less

Total Problems	35
Problems Correct	___

$10 - 8 = 2$

$4 - 1 = 3$	$7 - 6 = 1$	$10 - 5 = 5$
$5 - 0 = 5$	$6 - 4 = 2$	$8 - 0 = 8$
$10 - 6 = 4$	$8 - 2 = 6$	$5 - 2 = 3$
$6 - 1 = 5$	$7 - 5 = 2$	$3 - 3 = 0$
$10 - 4 = 6$	$4 - 2 = 2$	$9 - 4 = 5$
$9 - 6 = 3$	$5 - 3 = 2$	$10 - 10 = 0$
$8 - 3 = 5$	$8 - 1 = 7$	$6 - 2 = 4$
$9 - 3 = 6$	$6 - 3 = 3$	$1 - 1 = 0$
$8 - 8 = 0$	$2 - 2 = 0$	$10 - 7 = 3$
$10 - 1 = 9$	$9 - 5 = 4$	$7 - 3 = 4$
$1 - 0 = 1$	$6 - 6 = 0$	
$3 - 2 = 1$	$7 - 2 = 5$	

Practice brings success!

Page 56

Math IF8739

116

Answer Key

Subtraction

Skill: Subtraction From 10 or Less

Name _____

Total Problems ___35___

Problems Correct _____

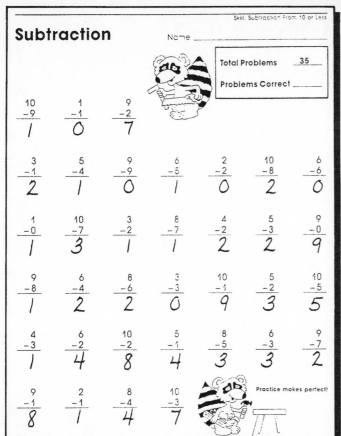

10 −9 1	1 −1 0	9 −2 7				
3 −1 2	5 −4 1	9 −9 0	6 −5 1	2 −2 0	10 −8 2	6 −6 0
1 −0 1	10 −7 3	3 −2 1	8 −7 1	4 −2 2	5 −3 2	9 −0 9
9 −8 1	6 −4 2	8 −6 2	3 −3 0	10 −1 9	5 −2 3	10 −5 5
4 −3 1	6 −2 4	10 −2 8	5 −1 4	8 −5 3	6 −3 3	9 −7 2
9 −1 8	2 −1 1	8 −4 4	10 −3 7			

Practice makes perfect!

Page 57

Subtraction

Skill: Subtraction From 11 or Less

Name _____

Total Problems ___25___

Problems Correct _____

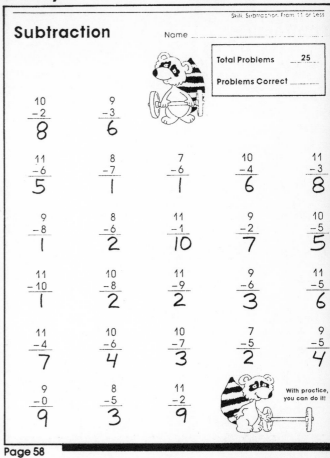

10 −2 8	9 −3 6			
11 −6 5	8 −7 1	7 −6 1	10 −4 6	11 −3 8
9 −8 1	8 −6 2	11 −1 10	9 −2 7	10 −5 5
11 −10 1	10 −8 2	11 −9 2	9 −6 3	11 −5 6
11 −4 7	10 −6 4	10 −7 3	7 −5 2	9 −5 4
9 −0 9	8 −5 3	11 −2 9		

With practice, you can do it!

Page 58

Subtraction

Skill: Subtraction From 11 or Less

Name _____

Total Problems ___30___

Problems Correct _____

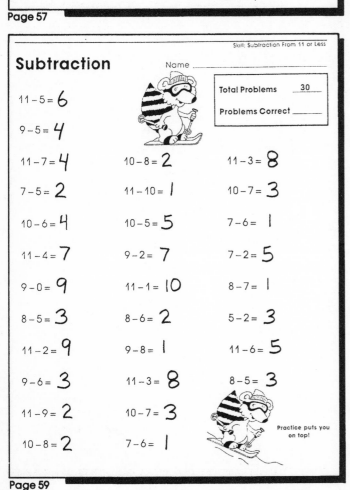

11 − 5 = 6

9 − 5 = 4

11 − 7 = 4   10 − 8 = 2   11 − 3 = 8

7 − 5 = 2   11 − 10 = 1   10 − 7 = 3

10 − 6 = 4   10 − 5 = 5   7 − 6 = 1

11 − 4 = 7   9 − 2 = 7   7 − 2 = 5

9 − 0 = 9   11 − 1 = 10   8 − 7 = 1

8 − 5 = 3   8 − 6 = 2   5 − 2 = 3

11 − 2 = 9   9 − 8 = 1   11 − 6 = 5

9 − 6 = 3   11 − 3 = 8   8 − 5 = 3

11 − 9 = 2   10 − 7 = 3

10 − 8 = 2   7 − 6 = 1

Practice puts you on top!

Page 59

Subtraction

Skill: Subtraction From 12 or Less

Name _____

Total Problems ___25___

Problems Correct _____

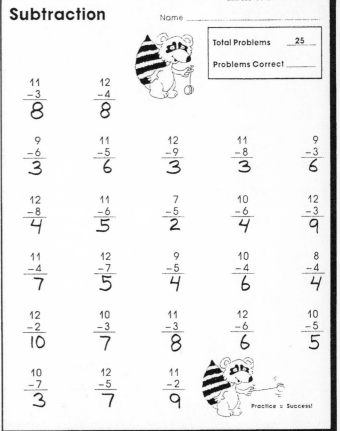

11 −3 8	12 −4 8			
9 −6 3	11 −5 6	12 −9 3	11 −8 3	9 −3 6
12 −8 4	11 −6 5	7 −5 2	10 −6 4	12 −3 9
11 −4 7	12 −7 5	9 −5 4	10 −4 6	8 −4 4
12 −2 10	10 −3 7	11 −3 8	12 −6 6	10 −5 5
10 −7 3	12 −5 7	11 −2 9		

Practice = Success!

Page 60

Answer Key

Subtraction

Name _____

Total Problems __30__

Problems Correct _____

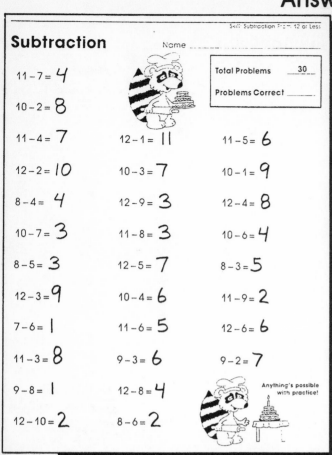

11 – 7 = 4

10 – 2 = 8

11 – 4 = 7   12 – 1 = 11   11 – 5 = 6

12 – 2 = 10   10 – 3 = 7   10 – 1 = 9

8 – 4 = 4   12 – 9 = 3   12 – 4 = 8

10 – 7 = 3   11 – 8 = 3   10 – 6 = 4

8 – 5 = 3   12 – 5 = 7   8 – 3 = 5

12 – 3 = 9   10 – 4 = 6   11 – 9 = 2

7 – 6 = 1   11 – 6 = 5   12 – 6 = 6

11 – 3 = 8   9 – 3 = 6   9 – 2 = 7

9 – 8 = 1   12 – 8 = 4

12 – 10 = 2   8 – 6 = 2

Anything's possible with practice!

Page 61

Subtraction

Name _____

Total Problems __25__

Problems Correct _____

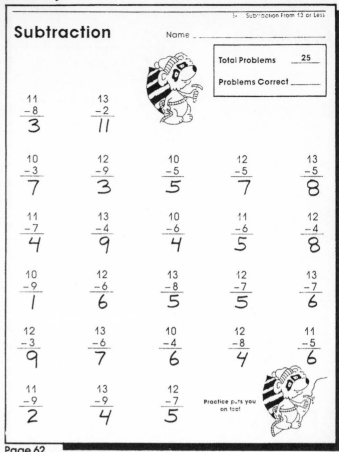

11 – 8 **3**	13 – 2 **11**			
10 – 3 **7**	12 – 9 **3**	10 – 5 **5**	12 – 5 **7**	13 – 5 **8**
11 – 7 **4**	13 – 4 **9**	10 – 6 **4**	11 – 6 **5**	12 – 4 **8**
10 – 9 **1**	12 – 6 **6**	13 – 8 **5**	12 – 7 **5**	13 – 7 **6**
12 – 3 **9**	13 – 6 **7**	10 – 4 **6**	12 – 8 **4**	11 – 5 **6**
11 – 9 **2**	13 – 9 **4**	12 – 7 **5**		

Practice puts you on ice!

Page 62

Subtraction

Name _____

Total Problems __25__

Problems Correct _____

12 – 6 **6**	14 – 9 **5**			
10 – 6 **4**	14 – 5 **9**	11 – 7 **4**	13 – 8 **5**	12 – 5 **7**
11 – 2 **9**	13 – 5 **8**	12 – 9 **3**	14 – 6 **8**	11 – 8 **3**
13 – 6 **7**	12 – 8 **4**	13 – 7 **6**	14 – 4 **10**	14 – 2 **12**
10 – 4 **6**	12 – 7 **5**	10 – 8 **2**	14 – 7 **7**	13 – 9 **4**
11 – 9 **2**	14 – 8 **6**	13 – 4 **9**		

Practice = Success!

Page 63

Subtraction

Name _____

Total Problems __30__

Problems Correct _____

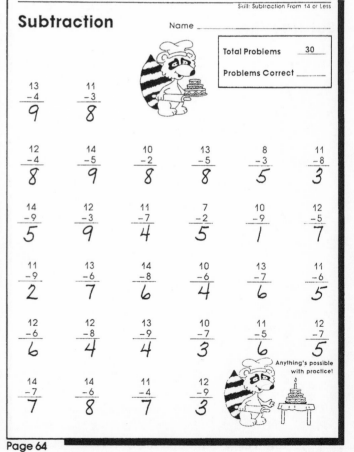

13 – 4 **9**	11 – 3 **8**				
12 – 4 **8**	14 – 5 **9**	10 – 2 **8**	13 – 5 **8**	8 – 3 **5**	11 – 8 **3**
14 – 9 **5**	12 – 3 **9**	11 – 7 **4**	7 – 2 **5**	10 – 9 **1**	12 – 5 **7**
11 – 9 **2**	13 – 6 **7**	14 – 8 **6**	10 – 6 **4**	13 – 7 **6**	11 – 6 **5**
12 – 6 **6**	12 – 8 **4**	13 – 9 **4**	10 – 7 **3**	11 – 5 **6**	12 – 7 **5**
14 – 7 **7**	14 – 6 **8**	11 – 4 **7**	12 – 9 **3**		

Anything's possible with practice!

Page 64

Answer Key

Page 65

Skill: Subtraction From 14 or Less

Subtraction

Name _____

Total Problems ___30___

Problems Correct _____

13 − 8 = 5	11 − 5 = 6				
12 − 4 = 8	13 − 5 = 8	14 − 9 = 5	9 − 6 = 3	12 − 8 = 4	11 − 2 = 9
11 − 7 = 4	12 − 7 = 5	13 − 9 = 4	10 − 5 = 5	12 − 5 = 7	13 − 6 = 7
14 − 7 = 7	10 − 3 = 7	11 − 3 = 8	12 − 9 = 3	14 − 8 = 6	8 − 4 = 4
13 − 7 = 6	6 − 3 = 3	10 − 4 = 6	12 − 3 = 9	11 − 6 = 5	14 − 5 = 9
14 − 6 = 8	11 − 4 = 7	12 − 6 = 6	13 − 4 = 9		

Practice = Success!

Page 66

Skill: Subtraction From 14 or Less

Subtraction

Name _____

Total Problems ___30___

Problems Correct _____

12 − 9 = 3	10 − 1 = 9				
14 − 9 = 5	11 − 2 = 9	13 − 9 = 4	8 − 5 = 3	12 − 4 = 8	13 − 6 = 7
7 − 4 = 3	11 − 9 = 2	14 − 8 = 6	10 − 8 = 2	12 − 3 = 9	11 − 3 = 8
13 − 8 = 5	13 − 4 = 9	12 − 8 = 4	13 − 7 = 6	11 − 8 = 3	5 − 3 = 2
12 − 5 = 7	14 − 7 = 7	11 − 7 = 4	9 − 7 = 2	13 − 5 = 8	12 − 7 = 5
11 − 6 = 5	14 − 6 = 8	6 − 2 = 4	12 − 6 = 6		

Practice puts you on top!

Page 67

Skill: Subtraction From 15 or Less

Subtraction

Name _____

Total Problems ___25___

Problems Correct _____

13 − 5 = 8	15 − 9 = 6			
10 − 4 = 6	14 − 6 = 8	13 − 6 = 7	10 − 9 = 1	15 − 7 = 8
12 − 5 = 7	15 − 5 = 10	13 − 7 = 6	12 − 7 = 5	10 − 6 = 4
11 − 6 = 5	12 − 4 = 8	15 − 6 = 9	13 − 9 = 4	14 − 5 = 9
12 − 9 = 3	13 − 8 = 5	14 − 7 = 7	12 − 6 = 6	15 − 9 = 6
10 − 5 = 5	15 − 8 = 7	12 − 8 = 4		

Practice hard. You'll win.

Page 68

Skill: Subtraction From 10 Through 18

Subtraction

Name _____

Total Problems ___30___

Problems Correct _____

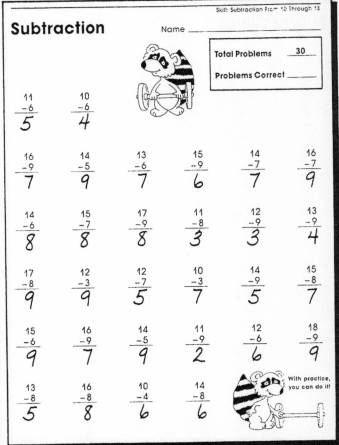

11 − 6 = 5	10 − 6 = 4				
16 − 9 = 7	14 − 5 = 9	13 − 6 = 7	15 − 9 = 6	14 − 7 = 7	16 − 7 = 9
14 − 6 = 8	15 − 7 = 8	17 − 9 = 8	11 − 8 = 3	12 − 9 = 3	13 − 9 = 4
17 − 8 = 9	12 − 3 = 9	12 − 7 = 5	10 − 3 = 7	14 − 9 = 5	15 − 8 = 7
15 − 6 = 9	16 − 9 = 7	14 − 5 = 9	11 − 9 = 2	12 − 6 = 6	18 − 9 = 9
13 − 8 = 5	16 − 8 = 8	10 − 4 = 6	14 − 8 = 6		

With practice, you can do it!

Answer Key

Subtraction — Page 69

Name _____

Total Problems __30__

Problems Correct _____

$$\begin{array}{c}17\\-8\\\hline 9\end{array}\qquad\begin{array}{c}12\\-9\\\hline 3\end{array}$$

$$\begin{array}{c}10\\-8\\\hline 2\end{array}\quad\begin{array}{c}11\\-2\\\hline 9\end{array}\quad\begin{array}{c}16\\-8\\\hline 8\end{array}\quad\begin{array}{c}14\\-9\\\hline 5\end{array}\quad\begin{array}{c}11\\-8\\\hline 3\end{array}\quad\begin{array}{c}12\\-6\\\hline 6\end{array}$$

$$\begin{array}{c}13\\-8\\\hline 5\end{array}\quad\begin{array}{c}15\\-9\\\hline 6\end{array}\quad\begin{array}{c}11\\-3\\\hline 8\end{array}\quad\begin{array}{c}14\\-5\\\hline 9\end{array}\quad\begin{array}{c}17\\-9\\\hline 8\end{array}\quad\begin{array}{c}12\\-8\\\hline 4\end{array}$$

$$\begin{array}{c}13\\-4\\\hline 9\end{array}\quad\begin{array}{c}16\\-7\\\hline 9\end{array}\quad\begin{array}{c}14\\-8\\\hline 6\end{array}\quad\begin{array}{c}18\\-9\\\hline 9\end{array}\quad\begin{array}{c}12\\-5\\\hline 7\end{array}\quad\begin{array}{c}15\\-6\\\hline 9\end{array}$$

$$\begin{array}{c}14\\-7\\\hline 7\end{array}\quad\begin{array}{c}10\\-2\\\hline 8\end{array}\quad\begin{array}{c}15\\-7\\\hline 8\end{array}\quad\begin{array}{c}13\\-9\\\hline 4\end{array}\quad\begin{array}{c}11\\-9\\\hline 2\end{array}\quad\begin{array}{c}13\\-7\\\hline 6\end{array}$$

$$\begin{array}{c}10\\-5\\\hline 5\end{array}\quad\begin{array}{c}16\\-9\\\hline 7\end{array}\quad\begin{array}{c}15\\-8\\\hline 7\end{array}\quad\begin{array}{c}14\\-6\\\hline 8\end{array}$$

Success ahoy! Just practice!

Page 69

Subtraction — Page 70

Name _____

Total Problems __30__

Problems Correct _____

$15-6=9$

$11-5=6$

$13-8=5 \qquad 18-9=9 \qquad 14-9=5$

$12-3=9 \qquad 10-5=5 \qquad 16-8=8$

$10-1=9 \qquad 11-4=7 \qquad 10-2=8$

$17-9=8 \qquad 11-2=9 \qquad 17-8=9$

$15-7=8 \qquad 13-7=6 \qquad 11-7=4$

$14-8=6 \qquad 12-6=6 \qquad 13-5=8$

$12-9=3 \qquad 10-9=1 \qquad 10-8=2$

$15-8=7 \qquad 14-6=8 \qquad 12-4=8$

$16-7=9 \qquad 15-9=6$

$12-5=7 \qquad 11-8=3$

Practice hard. You'll win.

Page 70

Subtraction — Page 71

Name _____

Total Problems __25__

Problems Correct _____

$$\begin{array}{c}15\\-10\\\hline 5\end{array}\qquad\begin{array}{c}83\\-52\\\hline 31\end{array}$$

$$\begin{array}{c}69\\-45\\\hline 24\end{array}\quad\begin{array}{c}64\\-41\\\hline 23\end{array}\quad\begin{array}{c}42\\-11\\\hline 31\end{array}\quad\begin{array}{c}39\\-16\\\hline 23\end{array}\quad\begin{array}{c}53\\-30\\\hline 23\end{array}$$

$$\begin{array}{c}78\\-45\\\hline 33\end{array}\quad\begin{array}{c}85\\-52\\\hline 33\end{array}\quad\begin{array}{c}90\\-40\\\hline 50\end{array}\quad\begin{array}{c}88\\-11\\\hline 77\end{array}\quad\begin{array}{c}78\\-35\\\hline 43\end{array}$$

$$\begin{array}{c}86\\-53\\\hline 33\end{array}\quad\begin{array}{c}57\\-46\\\hline 11\end{array}\quad\begin{array}{c}53\\-33\\\hline 20\end{array}\quad\begin{array}{c}64\\-41\\\hline 23\end{array}\quad\begin{array}{c}63\\-60\\\hline 3\end{array}$$

$$\begin{array}{c}75\\-31\\\hline 44\end{array}\quad\begin{array}{c}69\\-36\\\hline 33\end{array}\quad\begin{array}{c}77\\-52\\\hline 25\end{array}\quad\begin{array}{c}86\\-35\\\hline 51\end{array}\quad\begin{array}{c}58\\-28\\\hline 30\end{array}$$

$$\begin{array}{c}50\\-10\\\hline 40\end{array}\quad\begin{array}{c}86\\-55\\\hline 31\end{array}\quad\begin{array}{c}49\\-26\\\hline 23\end{array}$$

Through practice you learn!

Page 71

Subtraction — Page 72

Name _____

Total Problems __25__

Problems Correct _____

$$\begin{array}{c}86\\-54\\\hline 32\end{array}\qquad\begin{array}{c}60\\-30\\\hline 30\end{array}$$

$$\begin{array}{c}67\\-23\\\hline 44\end{array}\quad\begin{array}{c}74\\-45\\\hline 31\end{array}\quad\begin{array}{c}88\\-11\\\hline 77\end{array}\quad\begin{array}{c}47\\-17\\\hline 30\end{array}\quad\begin{array}{c}72\\-41\\\hline 31\end{array}$$

$$\begin{array}{c}66\\-23\\\hline 43\end{array}\quad\begin{array}{c}85\\-42\\\hline 43\end{array}\quad\begin{array}{c}38\\-28\\\hline 10\end{array}\quad\begin{array}{c}69\\-36\\\hline 33\end{array}\quad\begin{array}{c}99\\-40\\\hline 59\end{array}$$

$$\begin{array}{c}75\\-33\\\hline 42\end{array}\quad\begin{array}{c}67\\-62\\\hline 5\end{array}\quad\begin{array}{c}78\\-35\\\hline 43\end{array}\quad\begin{array}{c}65\\-41\\\hline 24\end{array}\quad\begin{array}{c}87\\-62\\\hline 25\end{array}$$

$$\begin{array}{c}50\\-10\\\hline 40\end{array}\quad\begin{array}{c}83\\-72\\\hline 11\end{array}\quad\begin{array}{c}96\\-23\\\hline 73\end{array}\quad\begin{array}{c}37\\-24\\\hline 13\end{array}\quad\begin{array}{c}80\\-30\\\hline 50\end{array}$$

$$\begin{array}{c}65\\-42\\\hline 23\end{array}\quad\begin{array}{c}38\\-16\\\hline 22\end{array}\quad\begin{array}{c}48\\-38\\\hline 10\end{array}$$

Practice and anything's possible!

Page 72

Answer Key

Page 73

Subtraction

Name _____

Total Problems **25**

Problems Correct _____

64 − 40 = **24**	87 − 12 = **75**			
81 − 21 = **60**	48 − 27 = **21**	83 − 41 = **42**	70 − 20 = **50**	66 − 33 = **33**
28 − 15 = **13**	98 − 54 = **44**	55 − 21 = **34**	86 − 82 = **4**	74 − 52 = **22**
78 − 62 = **16**	35 − 25 = **10**	69 − 23 = **46**	94 − 43 = **51**	49 − 20 = **29**
59 − 16 = **43**	86 − 34 = **52**	39 − 12 = **27**	88 − 10 = **78**	72 − 41 = **31**
67 − 32 = **35**	97 − 15 = **82**	26 − 13 = **13**		

Practice! Practice! Practice!

Page 73

Page 74

Subtraction

Name _____

Total Problems **25**

Problems Correct _____

56 − 42 = **14**	99 − 64 = **35**			
78 − 34 = **44**	33 − 12 = **21**	74 − 72 = **2**	66 − 30 = **36**	39 − 26 = **13**
98 − 25 = **73**	88 − 47 = **41**	61 − 31 = **30**	87 − 33 = **54**	48 − 43 = **5**
66 − 11 = **55**	97 − 27 = **70**	83 − 21 = **62**	28 − 10 = **18**	59 − 22 = **37**
79 − 35 = **44**	50 − 40 = **10**	47 − 24 = **23**	95 − 15 = **80**	65 − 32 = **33**
29 − 25 = **4**	96 − 13 = **83**	92 − 61 = **31**		

With practice, you can do it!

Page 74

Page 75

Subtraction

Name _____

Total Problems **25**

Problems Correct _____

66 − 19 = **47**	92 − 49 = **43**			
40 − 13 = **27**	74 − 57 = **17**	53 − 44 = **9**	30 − 15 = **15**	61 − 28 = **33**
95 − 36 = **59**	87 − 48 = **39**	52 − 16 = **36**	73 − 26 = **47**	24 − 18 = **6**
63 − 25 = **38**	21 − 17 = **4**	41 − 29 = **12**	50 − 26 = **24**	97 − 39 = **58**
76 − 59 = **17**	93 − 37 = **56**	65 − 39 = **26**	96 − 47 = **49**	85 − 27 = **58**
34 − 19 = **15**	42 − 18 = **24**	81 − 49 = **32**		

Page 75

Page 76

Subtraction

Name _____

Total Problems **25**

Problems Correct _____

71 − 54 = **17**	43 − 19 = **24**			
46 − 29 = **17**	81 − 36 = **45**	57 − 39 = **18**	90 − 18 = **72**	26 − 18 = **8**
81 − 12 = **69**	94 − 37 = **57**	43 − 24 = **19**	73 − 28 = **45**	82 − 35 = **47**
57 − 28 = **29**	91 − 26 = **65**	74 − 19 = **55**	62 − 13 = **49**	33 − 27 = **6**
88 − 29 = **59**	74 − 35 = **39**	65 − 38 = **27**	83 − 29 = **54**	60 − 36 = **24**
91 − 45 = **46**	52 − 24 = **28**	80 − 49 = **31**		

Practice = Success!

Page 76

Answer Key

Page 77

Subtraction

Name _____

Total Problems	25
Problems Correct	___

$\begin{array}{r} 55 \\ -26 \\ \hline 29 \end{array}$ $\begin{array}{r} 71 \\ -23 \\ \hline 48 \end{array}$

$\begin{array}{r} 92 \\ -37 \\ \hline 55 \end{array}$ $\begin{array}{r} 43 \\ -28 \\ \hline 15 \end{array}$ $\begin{array}{r} 90 \\ -36 \\ \hline 54 \end{array}$ $\begin{array}{r} 66 \\ -47 \\ \hline 19 \end{array}$ $\begin{array}{r} 25 \\ -19 \\ \hline 6 \end{array}$

$\begin{array}{r} 93 \\ -25 \\ \hline 68 \end{array}$ $\begin{array}{r} 98 \\ -49 \\ \hline 49 \end{array}$ $\begin{array}{r} 38 \\ -19 \\ \hline 19 \end{array}$ $\begin{array}{r} 41 \\ -27 \\ \hline 14 \end{array}$ $\begin{array}{r} 77 \\ -49 \\ \hline 28 \end{array}$

$\begin{array}{r} 62 \\ -23 \\ \hline 39 \end{array}$ $\begin{array}{r} 44 \\ -18 \\ \hline 26 \end{array}$ $\begin{array}{r} 76 \\ -29 \\ \hline 47 \end{array}$ $\begin{array}{r} 90 \\ -11 \\ \hline 79 \end{array}$ $\begin{array}{r} 72 \\ -16 \\ \hline 56 \end{array}$

$\begin{array}{r} 47 \\ -38 \\ \hline 9 \end{array}$ $\begin{array}{r} 85 \\ -47 \\ \hline 38 \end{array}$ $\begin{array}{r} 80 \\ -37 \\ \hline 43 \end{array}$ $\begin{array}{r} 51 \\ -38 \\ \hline 13 \end{array}$ $\begin{array}{r} 64 \\ -26 \\ \hline 38 \end{array}$

$\begin{array}{r} 83 \\ -77 \\ \hline 6 \end{array}$ $\begin{array}{r} 92 \\ -28 \\ \hline 64 \end{array}$ $\begin{array}{r} 97 \\ -68 \\ \hline 29 \end{array}$

Page 77

Page 78

Subtraction

Name _____

Total Problems	25
Problems Correct	___

$\begin{array}{r} 61 \\ -47 \\ \hline 14 \end{array}$ $\begin{array}{r} 78 \\ -33 \\ \hline 45 \end{array}$

$\begin{array}{r} 64 \\ -40 \\ \hline 24 \end{array}$ $\begin{array}{r} 28 \\ -19 \\ \hline 9 \end{array}$ $\begin{array}{r} 45 \\ -12 \\ \hline 33 \end{array}$ $\begin{array}{r} 77 \\ -29 \\ \hline 48 \end{array}$ $\begin{array}{r} 49 \\ -38 \\ \hline 11 \end{array}$

$\begin{array}{r} 89 \\ -83 \\ \hline 6 \end{array}$ $\begin{array}{r} 62 \\ -58 \\ \hline 4 \end{array}$ $\begin{array}{r} 75 \\ -25 \\ \hline 50 \end{array}$ $\begin{array}{r} 91 \\ -33 \\ \hline 58 \end{array}$ $\begin{array}{r} 30 \\ -19 \\ \hline 11 \end{array}$

$\begin{array}{r} 56 \\ -28 \\ \hline 28 \end{array}$ $\begin{array}{r} 92 \\ -35 \\ \hline 57 \end{array}$ $\begin{array}{r} 80 \\ -11 \\ \hline 69 \end{array}$ $\begin{array}{r} 27 \\ -17 \\ \hline 10 \end{array}$ $\begin{array}{r} 98 \\ -49 \\ \hline 49 \end{array}$

$\begin{array}{r} 93 \\ -86 \\ \hline 7 \end{array}$ $\begin{array}{r} 51 \\ -20 \\ \hline 31 \end{array}$ $\begin{array}{r} 98 \\ -42 \\ \hline 56 \end{array}$ $\begin{array}{r} 94 \\ -65 \\ \hline 29 \end{array}$ $\begin{array}{r} 86 \\ -22 \\ \hline 64 \end{array}$

$\begin{array}{r} 70 \\ -10 \\ \hline 60 \end{array}$ $\begin{array}{r} 85 \\ -16 \\ \hline 69 \end{array}$ $\begin{array}{r} 64 \\ -47 \\ \hline 17 \end{array}$

With practice, you can do it!

Page 78

Page 79

Subtraction

Name _____

Total Problems	25
Problems Correct	___

$\begin{array}{r} 78 \\ -19 \\ \hline 59 \end{array}$ $\begin{array}{r} 85 \\ -39 \\ \hline 46 \end{array}$

$\begin{array}{r} 46 \\ -36 \\ \hline 10 \end{array}$ $\begin{array}{r} 65 \\ -28 \\ \hline 37 \end{array}$ $\begin{array}{r} 92 \\ -49 \\ \hline 43 \end{array}$ $\begin{array}{r} 27 \\ -19 \\ \hline 8 \end{array}$ $\begin{array}{r} 74 \\ -22 \\ \hline 52 \end{array}$

$\begin{array}{r} 51 \\ -27 \\ \hline 24 \end{array}$ $\begin{array}{r} 63 \\ -36 \\ \hline 27 \end{array}$ $\begin{array}{r} 80 \\ -15 \\ \hline 65 \end{array}$ $\begin{array}{r} 97 \\ -64 \\ \hline 33 \end{array}$ $\begin{array}{r} 56 \\ -48 \\ \hline 8 \end{array}$

$\begin{array}{r} 44 \\ -29 \\ \hline 15 \end{array}$ $\begin{array}{r} 79 \\ -58 \\ \hline 21 \end{array}$ $\begin{array}{r} 87 \\ -48 \\ \hline 39 \end{array}$ $\begin{array}{r} 34 \\ -26 \\ \hline 8 \end{array}$ $\begin{array}{r} 94 \\ -15 \\ \hline 79 \end{array}$

$\begin{array}{r} 90 \\ -34 \\ \hline 56 \end{array}$ $\begin{array}{r} 53 \\ -45 \\ \hline 8 \end{array}$ $\begin{array}{r} 32 \\ -18 \\ \hline 14 \end{array}$ $\begin{array}{r} 89 \\ -12 \\ \hline 77 \end{array}$ $\begin{array}{r} 81 \\ -35 \\ \hline 46 \end{array}$

Practice brings success!

$\begin{array}{r} 78 \\ -43 \\ \hline 35 \end{array}$ $\begin{array}{r} 42 \\ -13 \\ \hline 29 \end{array}$ $\begin{array}{r} 50 \\ -30 \\ \hline 20 \end{array}$

Page 79

Page 80

Subtraction

Name _____

Total Problems	25
Problems Correct	___

$\begin{array}{r} 129 \\ -26 \\ \hline 103 \end{array}$ $\begin{array}{r} 976 \\ -432 \\ \hline 544 \end{array}$

$\begin{array}{r} 697 \\ -272 \\ \hline 425 \end{array}$ $\begin{array}{r} 458 \\ -141 \\ \hline 317 \end{array}$ $\begin{array}{r} 856 \\ -114 \\ \hline 742 \end{array}$ $\begin{array}{r} 379 \\ -163 \\ \hline 216 \end{array}$ $\begin{array}{r} 702 \\ -102 \\ \hline 600 \end{array}$

$\begin{array}{r} 216 \\ -13 \\ \hline 203 \end{array}$ $\begin{array}{r} 94 \\ -72 \\ \hline 22 \end{array}$ $\begin{array}{r} 885 \\ -330 \\ \hline 555 \end{array}$ $\begin{array}{r} 196 \\ -81 \\ \hline 115 \end{array}$ $\begin{array}{r} 98 \\ -46 \\ \hline 52 \end{array}$

$\begin{array}{r} 678 \\ -162 \\ \hline 516 \end{array}$ $\begin{array}{r} 327 \\ -23 \\ \hline 304 \end{array}$ $\begin{array}{r} 180 \\ -140 \\ \hline 40 \end{array}$ $\begin{array}{r} 997 \\ -354 \\ \hline 643 \end{array}$ $\begin{array}{r} 364 \\ -60 \\ \hline 304 \end{array}$

$\begin{array}{r} 111 \\ -10 \\ \hline 101 \end{array}$ $\begin{array}{r} 62 \\ -31 \\ \hline 31 \end{array}$ $\begin{array}{r} 143 \\ -23 \\ \hline 120 \end{array}$ $\begin{array}{r} 925 \\ -24 \\ \hline 901 \end{array}$ $\begin{array}{r} 300 \\ -100 \\ \hline 200 \end{array}$

$\begin{array}{r} 833 \\ -121 \\ \hline 712 \end{array}$ $\begin{array}{r} 278 \\ -60 \\ \hline 218 \end{array}$ $\begin{array}{r} 899 \\ -275 \\ \hline 624 \end{array}$

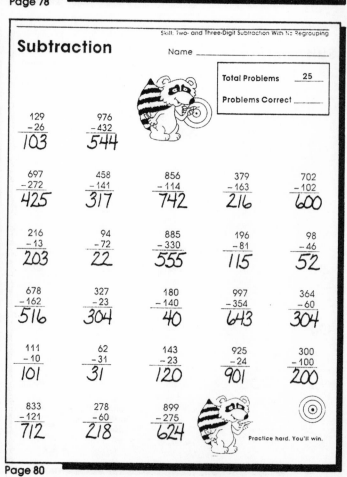

Practice hard. You'll win.

Page 80

Answer Key

Subtraction

Name _____

Total Problems ___25___

Problems Correct _____

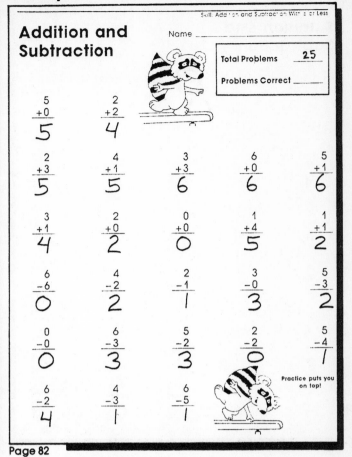

454 − 120 = **334**	675 − 125 = **550**			
158 − 147 = **11**	500 − 400 = **100**	996 − 413 = **583**	770 − 350 = **420**	195 − 181 = **14**
659 − 357 = **302**	332 − 111 = **221**	898 − 423 = **475**	297 − 152 = **145**	879 − 110 = **769**
780 − 130 = **650**	819 − 209 = **610**	529 − 216 = **313**	776 − 725 = **51**	490 − 360 = **130**
245 − 132 = **113**	657 − 122 = **535**	388 − 266 = **122**	427 − 212 = **215**	948 − 532 = **416**
730 − 130 = **600**	897 − 535 = **362**	968 − 721 = **247**		

Practice makes perfect!

Addition and Subtraction

Name _____

Total Problems ___25___

Problems Correct _____

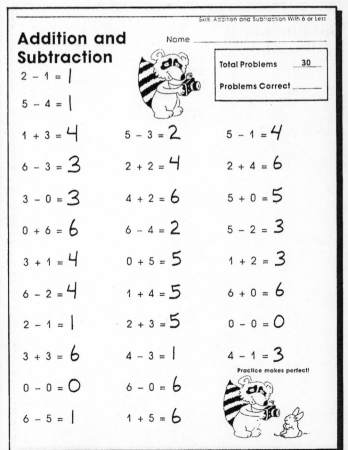

5 + 0 = **5**	2 + 2 = **4**			
2 + 3 = **5**	4 + 1 = **5**	3 + 3 = **6**	6 + 0 = **6**	5 + 1 = **6**
3 + 1 = **4**	2 + 0 = **2**	0 + 0 = **0**	1 + 4 = **5**	1 + 1 = **2**
6 − 6 = **0**	4 − 2 = **2**	2 − 1 = **1**	3 − 0 = **3**	5 − 3 = **2**
0 − 0 = **0**	6 − 3 = **3**	5 − 2 = **3**	2 − 2 = **0**	5 − 4 = **1**
6 − 2 = **4**	4 − 3 = **1**	6 − 5 = **1**		

Practice puts you on top!

Addition and Subtraction

Name _____

Total Problems ___25___

Problems Correct _____

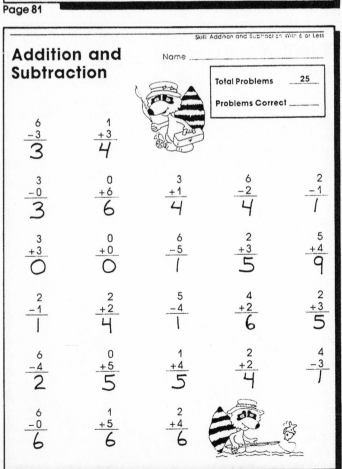

6 − 3 = **3**	1 + 3 = **4**			
3 − 0 = **3**	0 + 6 = **6**	3 + 1 = **4**	6 − 2 = **4**	2 − 1 = **1**
3 + 3 = **0**	0 + 0 = **0**	6 − 5 = **1**	2 + 3 = **5**	5 + 4 = **9**
2 − 1 = **1**	2 + 2 = **4**	5 − 4 = **1**	4 + 2 = **6**	2 + 3 = **5**
6 − 4 = **2**	0 + 5 = **5**	1 + 4 = **5**	2 + 2 = **4**	4 − 3 = **1**
6 − 0 = **6**	1 + 5 = **6**	2 + 4 = **6**		

Addition and Subtraction

Total Problems ___30___

Problems Correct _____

2 − 1 = **1**

5 − 4 = **1**

1 + 3 = **4**	5 − 3 = **2**	5 − 1 = **4**
6 − 3 = **3**	2 + 2 = **4**	2 + 4 = **6**
3 − 0 = **3**	4 + 2 = **6**	5 + 0 = **5**
0 + 6 = **6**	6 − 4 = **2**	5 − 2 = **3**
3 + 1 = **4**	0 + 5 = **5**	1 + 2 = **3**
6 − 2 = **4**	1 + 4 = **5**	6 + 0 = **6**
2 − 1 = **1**	2 + 3 = **5**	0 − 0 = **0**
3 + 3 = **6**	4 − 3 = **1**	4 − 1 = **3**
0 − 0 = **0**	6 − 0 = **6**	
6 − 5 = **1**	1 + 5 = **6**	

Practice makes perfect!

Answer Key

Addition and Subtraction

Name _____

Total Problems	25
Problems Correct	_____

3 + 5 = **8**   9 + 1 = **10**

6 + 3 = **9**   8 + 2 = **10**   7 + 3 = **10**   6 + 2 = **8**   7 + 1 = **8**

6 + 4 = **10**   9 + 0 = **9**   4 + 4 = **8**   8 + 1 = **9**   5 + 4 = **9**

9 − 5 = **4**   6 − 2 = **4**   8 − 5 = **3**   10 − 2 = **8**   7 − 7 = **0**

6 − 3 = **3**   5 − 1 = **4**   9 − 0 = **9**   10 − 5 = **5**   9 − 6 = **3**

Practice and anything's possible!

8 − 4 = **4**   10 − 6 = **4**   9 − 4 = **5**

Page 85

Addition and Subtraction

Name _____

Total Problems	25
Problems Correct	_____

6 + 4 = **10**   9 − 3 = **6**

5 + 5 = **10**   8 − 2 = **6**   10 − 4 = **6**   2 + 7 = **9**   8 − 5 = **3**

9 − 6 = **3**   5 + 3 = **8**   9 − 4 = **5**   8 + 2 = **10**   7 − 4 = **3**

6 + 3 = **9**   10 − 10 = **0**   5 + 1 = **6**   5 + 4 = **9**   5 − 4 = **1**

10 − 4 = **6**   7 + 3 = **10**   2 + 6 = **8**   8 − 7 = **1**   6 − 3 = **3**

Through practice you learn!

9 + 1 = **10**   8 − 4 = **4**   3 + 4 = **7**

Page 86

Addition and Subtraction

Name _____

Total Problems	30
Problems Correct	_____

8 − 4 = **4**

6 + 3 = **9**

10 − 10 = **0**   3 + 4 = **7**   5 + 4 = **9**

5 + 1 = **6**   5 + 5 = **10**   6 − 4 = **2**

4 + 5 = **9**   8 − 2 = **6**   7 + 3 = **10**

5 − 4 = **1**   10 − 6 = **4**   9 − 2 = **7**

10 − 4 = **6**   2 + 7 = **9**   8 − 6 = **2**

7 + 3 = **10**   8 − 5 = **3**   5 + 3 = **8**

2 + 6 = **8**   6 + 4 = **10**   10 − 0 = **10**

8 − 7 = **1**   9 − 3 = **6**   9 − 1 = **8**

6 − 3 = **3**   10 − 10 = **0**

9 + 1 = **10**   5 + 1 = **6**

Practice hard. You'll win.

Page 87

Addition and Subtraction

Name _____

Total Problems	35
Problems Correct	_____

6 + 3 = **9**   8 − 1 = **7**   5 − 2 = **3**

4 + 3 = **7**   10 − 7 = **3**   1 + 5 = **6**   6 − 3 = **3**   5 − 1 = **4**   0 + 7 = **7**   2 + 1 = **3**

9 − 6 = **3**   4 − 2 = **2**   5 + 5 = **10**   7 − 5 = **2**   8 − 6 = **2**   2 + 7 = **9**   5 − 2 = **3**

7 − 4 = **3**   2 + 3 = **5**   9 − 8 = **1**   5 + 2 = **7**   6 − 2 = **4**   3 − 1 = **2**   2 + 8 = **10**

4 + 2 = **6**   6 − 4 = **2**   8 − 4 = **4**   5 + 3 = **8**   9 − 5 = **4**   4 + 4 = **8**   10 − 5 = **5**

Practice! Practice! Practice!

4 + 1 = **5**   8 − 0 = **8**   7 − 7 = **0**   1 + 9 = **10**

Page 88

Math IF8739

124

© 1990 Instructional Fair, Inc.

Answer Key

Addition and Subtraction

Name _____

Total Problems **25**

Problems Correct _____

10 − 5 = **5**	9 + 2 = **11**			
9 − 2 = **7**	4 + 7 = **11**	5 + 6 = **11**	11 − 9 = **2**	10 − 6 = **4**
7 + 1 = **8**	8 + 3 = **11**	11 − 7 = **4**	10 − 4 = **6**	5 + 5 = **10**
8 + 2 = **10**	10 + 1 = **11**	11 − 4 = **7**	7 + 3 = **10**	10 − 3 = **7**
10 − 7 = **3**	11 − 6 = **5**	6 + 4 = **10**	10 − 8 = **2**	7 + 3 = **10**
9 + 1 = **10**	11 − 2 = **9**	5 + 4 = **9**		

Practice makes perfect!

Page 89

Addition and Subtraction

Name _____

Total Problems **25**

Problems Correct _____

7 + 4 = **11**	12 − 6 = **6**			
3 + 8 = **11**	6 + 6 = **12**	12 − 4 = **8**	5 + 5 = **10**	11 − 3 = **8**
11 − 6 = **5**	9 + 2 = **11**	7 + 5 = **12**	12 − 3 = **9**	8 + 2 = **10**
10 − 4 = **6**	6 + 5 = **11**	12 − 2 = **10**	7 + 3 = **10**	11 − 5 = **6**
11 − 7 = **4**	8 + 4 = **12**	10 − 7 = **3**	9 + 3 = **12**	11 − 8 = **3**
5 + 5 = **10**	12 − 5 = **7**	11 − 4 = **7**		

Practice brings success!

Page 90

Addition and Subtraction

Name _____

Total Problems **30**

Problems Correct _____

1 + 9 = **10**	10 − 6 = **4**				
14 − 9 = **5**	3 + 8 = **11**	14 − 7 = **7**	6 + 4 = **10**	13 − 7 = **6**	2 + 9 = **11**
13 − 8 = **5**	3 + 9 = **12**	11 − 8 = **3**	8 + 5 = **13**	10 − 1 = **9**	12 − 6 = **6**
6 + 7 = **13**	11 − 6 = **5**	4 + 8 = **12**	10 − 2 = **8**	5 + 6 = **11**	12 − 3 = **9**
7 + 7 = **14**	12 − 5 = **7**	6 + 8 = **14**	5 + 9 = **14**	13 − 4 = **9**	5 + 7 = **12**
9 + 2 = **11**	9 + 4 = **13**	14 − 8 = **6**	12 − 7 = **5**		

Practice hard. You'll win!

Page 91

Addition and Subtraction

Name _____

Total Problems **30**

Problems Correct _____

15 − 9 = **6**	9 + 9 = **18**				
8 + 9 = **17**	17 − 9 = **8**	15 − 8 = **7**	11 − 2 = **9**	6 + 9 = **15**	16 − 7 = **9**
12 − 9 = **3**	6 + 7 = **13**	16 − 8 = **8**	7 + 8 = **15**	14 − 6 = **8**	9 + 2 = **11**
15 − 6 = **9**	8 + 8 = **16**	18 − 9 = **9**	9 + 3 = **12**	7 + 9 = **16**	13 − 5 = **8**
6 + 5 = **11**	8 + 6 = **14**	13 − 6 = **7**	9 + 7 = **16**	9 + 8 = **17**	15 − 7 = **8**
9 + 6 = **15**	17 − 8 = **9**	8 + 7 = **15**	16 − 9 = **7**		

Page 92

125

Answer Key

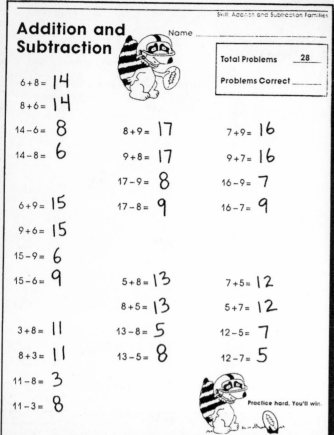

Skill: Addition and Subtraction Families

Addition and Subtraction

Name _____

Total Problems   28

Problems Correct _____

6 + 8 = 14

8 + 6 = 14

14 − 6 = 8

14 − 8 = 6

8 + 9 = 17   7 + 9 = 16

9 + 8 = 17   9 + 7 = 16

17 − 9 = 8   16 − 9 = 7

6 + 9 = 15

9 + 6 = 15

17 − 8 = 9   16 − 7 = 9

15 − 9 = 6

15 − 6 = 9

5 + 8 = 13   7 + 5 = 12

8 + 5 = 13   5 + 7 = 12

3 + 8 = 11

8 + 3 = 11   13 − 8 = 5   12 − 5 = 7

              13 − 5 = 8   12 − 7 = 5

11 − 8 = 3

11 − 3 = 8

Practice hard. You'll win.

Page 93

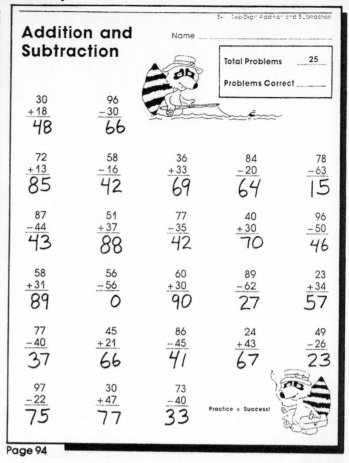

Skill: Two-Digit Addition and Subtraction

Addition and Subtraction

Name _____

Total Problems   25

Problems Correct _____

30	96			
+ 18	− 30			
48	66			

72	58	36	84	78
+ 13	− 16	+ 33	− 20	− 63
85	42	69	64	15

87	51	77	40	96
− 44	+ 37	− 35	+ 30	− 50
43	88	42	70	46

58	56	60	89	23
+ 31	− 56	+ 30	− 62	+ 34
89	0	90	27	57

77	45	86	24	49
− 40	+ 21	− 45	+ 43	− 26
37	66	41	67	23

97	30	73		
− 22	+ 47	− 40		
75	77	33		

Practice = Success!

Page 94

Skill: Two-Digit Addition and Subtraction

Addition and Subtraction

Name _____

Total Problems   25

Problems Correct _____

54	16			
+ 34	− 11			
88	5			

62	62	47	65	48
− 41	+ 20	+ 32	− 45	− 15
21	82	79	20	33

36	17	69	64	76
+ 40	+ 41	− 28	+ 32	− 52
76	58	41	96	24

86	50	32	83	60
− 62	− 30	+ 32	− 72	+ 20
24	20	64	11	80

88	61	35	87	
− 11	+ 38	+ 43	− 52	
77	99	78	35	

Practice! Practice! Practice!

30	45	62	40	
+ 29	− 42	+ 35	+ 29	
59	3	97	69	

Page 95

Skill: Two-Digit Addition and Subtraction

Addition and Subtraction

Name _____

Total Problems   25

Problems Correct _____

75	36			
− 25	+ 25			
50	61			

27	15	50	75	23
− 17	+ 19	− 22	− 37	+ 75
10	34	28	38	98

79	97	51	43	61
+ 10	− 84	+ 28	− 24	+ 19
89	13	79	19	80

96	82	33	66	86
− 18	− 46	+ 49	+ 22	− 24
78	36	82	88	62

62	29	39	53	80
− 19	+ 29	− 16	− 24	+ 12
43	58	23	29	92

Through practice you learn!

40	71	79		
+ 30	− 30	+ 18		
70	41	97		

Page 96

Answer Key

Addition and Subtraction

Name _____

Total Problems __25__

Problems Correct _____

66 −40 **26**	16 +19 **35**			
27 +16 **43**	88 −63 **25**	21 +71 **92**	91 −25 **66**	52 +37 **89**
83 +14 **97**	32 −17 **15**	59 −45 **14**	48 +47 **95**	70 −11 **59**
33 −15 **18**	41 +50 **91**	42 +37 **79**	97 −34 **63**	68 −49 **19**
76 +22 **98**	47 +13 **60**	59 +26 **85**	54 −27 **27**	24 −14 **10**
74 −50 **24**	79 +18 **97**	62 +23 **85**		

Practice hard
You'll win!

Page 97

Addition and Subtraction

Name _____

Total Problems __25__

Problems Correct _____

127 +611 **738**	932 −410 **522**			
319 −219 **100**	455 +102 **557**	840 −340 **500**	254 +515 **769**	821 −710 **111**
488 +400 **888**	671 −361 **310**	285 +214 **499**	178 −156 **22**	867 +131 **998**
376 +501 **877**	747 −632 **115**	163 +205 **368**	500 −300 **200**	612 +174 **786**
599 −127 **472**	253 +403 **656**	584 −241 **343**	326 +211 **537**	427 −227 **200**
550 −110 **440**	157 +132 **289**	737 −331 **406**		

Anything's possible
with practice!

Page 98

Multiplication

Name _____

Total Problems __25__

Problems Correct _____

0 ×3 **0**	2 ×1 **2**			
2 ×2 **4**	3 ×5 **15**	3 ×1 **3**	0 ×3 **0**	1 ×2 **2**
2 ×5 **10**	3 ×4 **12**	1 ×1 **1**	2 ×3 **6**	0 ×0 **0**
0 ×1 **0**	2 ×4 **8**	1 ×5 **5**	3 ×2 **6**	1 ×0 **0**
3 ×3 **9**	1 ×3 **3**	4 ×3 **12**	2 ×5 **10**	0 ×2 **0**
1 ×4 **4**	4 ×2 **8**	5 ×2 **10**		

Practice! Practice! Practice!

Page 99

Multiplication

Name _____

Total Problems __25__

Problems Correct _____

4 ×0 **0**	3 ×5 **15**			
3 ×3 **9**	5 ×1 **5**	4 ×3 **12**	3 ×1 **3**	4 ×5 **20**
3 ×0 **0**	4 ×2 **8**	5 ×4 **20**	3 ×2 **6**	5 ×3 **15**
3 ×3 **9**	4 ×3 **12**	3 ×2 **6**	5 ×0 **0**	4 ×1 **4**
5 ×2 **10**	4 ×3 **12**	5 ×1 **5**	3 ×4 **12**	4 ×0 **0**
3 ×0 **0**	5 ×5 **25**	4 ×4 **16**		

Practice and anything's possible!

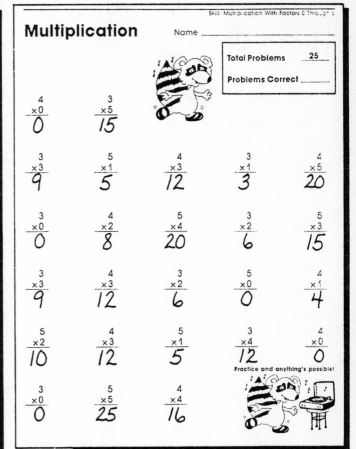

Page 100

Answer Key

Multiplication

Name _____

Skill: Multiplication With Factors 0 Through 5

Total Problems	30
Problems Correct	____

$\begin{array}{r}4\\ \times 3\\ \hline 12\end{array}$ $\quad$ $\begin{array}{r}2\\ \times 1\\ \hline 2\end{array}$

$\begin{array}{r}2\\ \times 4\\ \hline 8\end{array}$ $\begin{array}{r}1\\ \times 0\\ \hline 0\end{array}$ $\begin{array}{r}5\\ \times 3\\ \hline 15\end{array}$ $\begin{array}{r}4\\ \times 5\\ \hline 20\end{array}$ $\begin{array}{r}2\\ \times 0\\ \hline 0\end{array}$ $\begin{array}{r}3\\ \times 3\\ \hline 9\end{array}$

$\begin{array}{r}3\\ \times 1\\ \hline 3\end{array}$ $\begin{array}{r}5\\ \times 4\\ \hline 20\end{array}$ $\begin{array}{r}4\\ \times 2\\ \hline 8\end{array}$ $\begin{array}{r}1\\ \times 1\\ \hline 1\end{array}$ $\begin{array}{r}3\\ \times 5\\ \hline 15\end{array}$ $\begin{array}{r}1\\ \times 4\\ \hline 4\end{array}$

$\begin{array}{r}4\\ \times 1\\ \hline 4\end{array}$ $\begin{array}{r}2\\ \times 5\\ \hline 10\end{array}$ $\begin{array}{r}1\\ \times 5\\ \hline 5\end{array}$ $\begin{array}{r}3\\ \times 4\\ \hline 12\end{array}$ $\begin{array}{r}2\\ \times 3\\ \hline 6\end{array}$ $\begin{array}{r}5\\ \times 5\\ \hline 25\end{array}$

$\begin{array}{r}5\\ \times 2\\ \hline 10\end{array}$ $\begin{array}{r}3\\ \times 2\\ \hline 6\end{array}$ $\begin{array}{r}0\\ \times 1\\ \hline 0\end{array}$ $\begin{array}{r}5\\ \times 0\\ \hline 0\end{array}$ $\begin{array}{r}1\\ \times 2\\ \hline 2\end{array}$ $\begin{array}{r}4\\ \times 5\\ \hline 20\end{array}$

Practice = Success!

$\begin{array}{r}3\\ \times 0\\ \hline 0\end{array}$ $\begin{array}{r}2\\ \times 2\\ \hline 4\end{array}$ $\begin{array}{r}1\\ \times 3\\ \hline 3\end{array}$ $\begin{array}{r}5\\ \times 1\\ \hline 5\end{array}$

Multiplication

Name _____

Skill: Multiplication With Factors 0 Through 5

Total Problems	30
Problems Correct	____

$2 \times 1 = 2$

$4 \times 1 = 4$

$1 \times 1 = 1$ $\qquad$ $0 \times 0 = 0$ $\qquad$ $2 \times 5 = 10$

$0 \times 1 = 0$ $\qquad$ $3 \times 3 = 9$ $\qquad$ $4 \times 5 = 20$

$3 \times 5 = 15$ $\qquad$ $4 \times 4 = 16$ $\qquad$ $0 \times 4 = 0$

$4 \times 2 = 8$ $\qquad$ $1 \times 2 = 2$ $\qquad$ $2 \times 2 = 4$

$2 \times 4 = 8$ $\qquad$ $0 \times 5 = 0$ $\qquad$ $5 \times 2 = 10$

$3 \times 2 = 6$ $\qquad$ $2 \times 3 = 6$ $\qquad$ $1 \times 3 = 3$

$4 \times 3 = 12$ $\qquad$ $5 \times 3 = 15$ $\qquad$ $0 \times 2 = 0$

$0 \times 3 = 0$ $\qquad$ $5 \times 5 = 25$ $\qquad$ $3 \times 1 = 3$

$5 \times 4 = 20$ $\qquad$ $1 \times 4 = 4$

With practice, you can do it!

$1 \times 5 = 5$ $\qquad$ $3 \times 4 = 12$